THE ABRACADABRA KID

My first professional picture, at age thirteen. I look more
uncomfortable than the rabbit, which had never done
the rabbit-from-the-hat trick before. Neither had I. Soon
after, I learned that rabbits don't like to be lifted by the
ears, so I quit it.

THE ABRACADABRA KID

◄ A Writer's Life ►

SID FLEISCHMAN

Greenwillow Books, New York

Library of Congress Cataloging-in-Publication Data
Fleischman, Sid, (date)
The abracadabra kid : a writer's life / by Sid Fleischman.
p.   cm.
Summary: The autobiography of the Newbery award-winning
children's author who set out from childhood to be a magician.
ISBN 0-688-14859-X
1. Fleischman, Sid, (date)—Biography—Juvenile literature.
2. Authors, American—20th century—Biography—Juvenile literature.
3. Children's stories—Authorship—Juvenile literature.
[1. Fleischman, Sid, (date).   2. Authorship.]   I. Title.
PS3556.L42269Z462   1996   813'.54—dc20
[B]   95-47382   CIP   AC

FOR THE CAST OF PLAYERS

IN THESE PAGES, EACH

AND EVERY ONE, WITH

GRATITUDE AND AFFECTION

CONTENTS

THE ABRACADABRA KID

THE FATEFUL NICKEL

*Dear Sid Fleischman, I have read
Mr. Mysterious & Company. It's
the second best book I ever read.*

I am astonished, when I pause to think about it, to discover myself to be an author of humorous novels for children. Or an author at all. I had a childhood much like everyone else's. What went wrong?

Few kids aspire to be writers when they grow up. When we are young, authors are unseen, ghostly presences. They certainly didn't hang around my neighborhood in San Diego when I was growing up. I was in my early twenties before I saw a live author.

During the Second World War the U.S. Navy briefly stationed me in New York City. Late one afternoon I stepped into an elevator and there stood Carl Sandburg. I recognized him at once and promptly quick-froze. I wanted desperately to say something profound, such as "Hello, Mr. Sandburg," but I was unable to thaw out my voice. It was a hot, humid summer day, and I did notice that the great American poet and Lincoln biographer was perspiring. That was my first clue that authors were human, like the rest of us.

And alive. From time to time my publisher sends along a letter from a child inquiring how long Sid Fleischman has been dead. There seems to be a kind of childhood folklore that all authors are dead. Or ought to be.

The role modeling just isn't there.

I became a writer quite by accident. In school I was being properly formatted to become a productive member of society, but I decided to become a magician instead.

I was in the fifth grade. The Great Depression was a dismal year old. Even a child could sense that something was wrong, for many of the downtown shops had fallen dark as tombs. Still, San Diego, with its vast blue harbor, was luckier than most cities. It was the nesting place for the U.S. Navy Eleventh Fleet, and mercifully sailors on shore liberty had a few bucks to spend.

By a stroke of luck, my father, who'd been a child tailor in "the old country," had a shop on Fifth Avenue catering to sailor's needs—uniforms, boatswains' whistles, and other naval impedimenta. He was managing to survive, hanging on by his tobacco-stained fingernails.

One autumn day the large vacant store next door was hung like a stage set with gaudy canvas signs. A ten-in-one sideshow troop had moved in. The numbers described the procession of bizarre and wonderful features you could witness for a single admission.

My father gave me a fateful nickel to tour this storefront extravaganza, and my life changed forever. I was allowed past the velvet curtain. There, under the blazing lights, the first performer was about to drive a gleaming six-inch spike up his nose. I watched without the slightest inclination to go home and do likewise. What I envied about the spike man were the

A characteristic pose of me looking forward, as usual. Here
I am looking forward to my fourth birthday. Notice my
trend-setting haircut, which finally caught on in the 1990s.

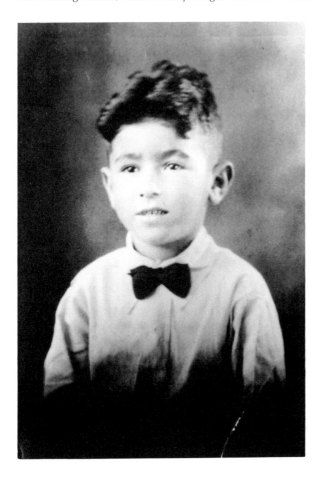

dove gray spats he wore tightly buckled over his shoes. They
struck me as worldly and theatrical.

I quickly learned that everyone in the ten-in-one doubled
or tripled as acts. The man with the spats, whose polka dot
blue bow tie kept bobbing above a restless Adam's apple,
became our guide through the wonders in the room. He intro-

duced a pretty young woman named Wanda, who could throw her voice into a scuffed suitcase and did a vent act with a red-headed dummy. She reappeared after the fat lady, this time climbing into a packing case. The man with the spats ran swords through the box, yet moments later indestructible Wanda hopped back into view without a scratch.

The two pinhead freaks disturbed me, with their puzzled, spider monkey faces, and I was glad to move on around the room. By time Wanda reappeared a last time, I was smitten. Not only was she enchanting, but Wanda was a show biz Renaissance woman, for now, slipping into a coat of fringed buckskin, she did a sharpshooting act. Decades later I was to draw on her in creating the character of the sharpshooting Arizona Girl in my novel *Jim Ugly*.

But there was one more act. The man with the spats rolled up his sleeves and proceeded to pluck a polished red billiard ball out of thin air. Presto! It vanished. Abracadabra! It reappeared. It turned white. It blushed red again. Voilà! Suddenly there were four billiard balls between this amazing man's fingers.

I was stunned. All of this was happening right under my nose. And there was more. He flipped the deck into falling waterfalls of cards, spun them into fans, and thrust a sword through a shower of cards to impale the seven of diamonds—selected a moment before.

I was dazzled. The moment he finished his act and ushered us gawkers back onto the sidewalk, I knew what I wanted to be. Someone else could be president of the United States.

I wanted to be a magician.

THE FLEDGLING MYSTIC

Dear Sid, I think for a man
you write pretty good books.

Now that my future was settled, all I had to do was discover how to conjure myself into a magician. At that time there was no school for wanna-be wizards in San Diego. No one gave private lessons. No dimly lit magic shop, selling secrets or paraphernalia, existed.

I had an idea. I'd ask my parents and aunts and uncles to teach me any tricks they knew. With their collective knowledge, I'd launch my career.

This plan proved to be an exercise in futility. My relatives, mostly émigrés from small villages in Russia, Poland, and Romania, didn't know how to pull coins from my ear or thrust swords through a girl-filled box.

I finally hit pay dirt when a passing friend showed me how to chew up a raisin thoroughly, flutter my fingers in the air, and withdraw from my lips the raisin restored.

You needed to snug a duplicate raisin under your lip and, after swallowing the first raisin, draw forth the duplicate. It wasn't exactly a showstopper. In fact it was a rotten trick. But I was desperate.

My father, meanwhile, having become friends with the impresario of the ten-in-one next door, let drop that the store-front Ziegfeld would let me see the show anytime—and free.

I was ecstatic. With a sort of lifetime pass, I'd hurry downtown after school to gaze at the man in the gray spats. He could make a half dollar tumble like a flashing silver acrobat across his knuckles. A red silk handkerchief, when drawn through his fist, fluttered out a brilliant cobalt blue.

I came to know him, and when he let me run errands for him, I no longer felt so much like a "townie"—a local. I was "with it." I was on the inside.

His name was Harry Snyder. He was no commonplace trickster. I soon discovered that he was a skilled and highly regarded sleight of hand man, banished by hard times to the show business slums. He'd learned to drive a stake up his nostril and to pitch carnival novelties and swindles for extra nickels and dimes.

One Saturday morning he sent me to a printshop to beg a handful of paper scraps. These he stamped with a blue keyhole and slipped into coin envelopes. At the next show I saw him peddle the keyholes for a twentieth part of a dollar.

"Gentlemen, see what Johnny saw when he peeked through the keyhole," said the professor of magic, his bow tie bobbing. "You have merely to hold this parchment up to a strong lightbulb, and view for yourself what Johnny saw through the keyhole. And after you look, my friends, sell the keyhole to a friend for a ten-cent piece and double your money."

I was just old enough to be kind of curious myself. What had the professor of magic done to the blank wastepaper I'd brought him? I held the keyhole to the light. I couldn't see anything.

Mr. Snyder might have laughed at my falling for this ancient pitch. Instead, with a carnival man's conspiratorial wink, he confessed. "That's what Johnny saw. Nothing."

He wasn't selling wastepaper. He was peddling imagination, a good-natured laugh—a dusty joke. It was my first lesson in presto chango, in which an audience can be happily led into fooling itself. And it turned me into a budding skeptic, for I'd also noticed there weren't ten acts in the ten-in-one show. I counted only nine.

Soon after, I hurried downtown after school and found the storefront deserted. The wonder show had rolled its splashy canvas banners and vanished into the night. The puzzle-eyed pinheads were gone. The sharpshooting Wanda was gone. And the magician in gray spats and bow tie had vanished, too. I felt abandoned. The ten-in-one left no footprints and was quickly forgotten, except by me.

Before he was gone, Mr. Snyder had shown me how to make a coin disappear. It was a giant step up from the raisin trick. About this time my mother's young brother, Nelson, only a few years older than I, moved to town and astonished me by reading off the pips of cards *by his fingertips*.

As he held each card before my eyes, he'd feel the face. "Ten of diamonds . . . three of clubs . . . king of hearts . . ."

My sister Pearl, standing beside him, began to laugh. She was seeing how it was done. I became more and more mystified and begged him to show me how to do it. Instead he gave the pack to Pearl, and *she* began to read off the cards with her fingertips. I was flabbergasted. She couldn't even do the raisin trick.

And then I noticed that she kept glancing over my shoulder. When I looked around, I saw that Uncle Nelson had backed me up to a mirror. For years I kept an eye out for hanging mirrors enabling me to repeat this great mystery. Alas, the only dependable venue for this trick turned out to be the bathroom. Eventually I learned to do it without mirrors. With sleight of hand. Easy.

I was as fascinated as everyone else by Houdini's fabled escapes. One day I was roaming about with my Bauman cousins, Seymour, my own age, and Jack, a few years younger. We decided to tie Jack up to a tree, like Houdini, and see if he could escape. And then, incomprehensibly, we ran off and left him. Jack must have escaped, because he grew up to be a top Santa Monica anesthesiologist.

With my mentor, Harry Snyder, vanished, I was left alone in my pursuit of things secret and mystic. I couldn't expect to find such arcane matters revealed in the public library, but I poked my head in. There, on a shelf, stood two boys' books of magic tricks. My heart skipped a beat. I knew at once that I'd scratched into a mother lode. Within the next few years I read every magic book on the shelves of the main library downtown and all of the outlying branches.

I was on the way to becoming a writer. I just didn't know it.

MAN OF AIR

Sorry I can't talk long,
but I'm planning to write
to the president.

There had never been a writer in my family. The men on both sides had been born to the needle trade, as poor tailors and pressers. Had my father not fled Russia, I no doubt would have grown up under the ancestral curse.

He was born in a shabby Ukrainian village named Olik (pronounced *o-leek*, and sometimes spelled Olyk or Olyka), a dusty speck on the road that has vanished from most contemporary maps. Huddling in the prairie shadow of the big city of Rovno, the village kept waking up through centuries of war to find itself in a different country. Without moving an inch, Olik has been a tourist in Poland, in Austria, in Poland again, in Russia, and back where it started, in the Ukraine.

When I was young, it confounded me that my father, whose name was Rivven, anglicized to Ruben, didn't know when he was born. The most important day of the year, and he didn't even know what *year*.

"Dad, how come Bubba didn't tell you when you were born?" I once asked. My grandmother was a birdlike, mis-

My father, on the left, shortly before he emigrated from the Old World to the New. He appears to have taken some pains to reveal the watch fob hanging from a vest pocket. Did he really own a watch? He made the suit himself, stitch by stitch. The young man seated was a boyhood friend, identity now unknown.

placed, and silent widow who wasn't adjusting to being uprooted and transplanted. She spoke no English.

He gave a small, bemused shrug. "What kind of *meshugge* [crazy] question is that? Of course she told me. The day after *mein* uncle Wolf fell in the river and almost drowned, the next day I was born. Who had calendars?"

I'd always known him as a man of the city, stylishly trim and nattily dressed. He wore two flashing gold teeth up front, capping the stumps left by the Russian practice of drinking tea through a lump of sugar held between the teeth.

It was hard to glimpse the village bumpkin who had washed up on the shores of Ellis Island in 1908. He became a New Yorker with the speed and flash of a quick-change artist. He almost instantly adopted the name Louie, regarding it as American as the Statue of Liberty. It was a name he heard everywhere on the streets of Manhattan, much as Bud or Mac came to be used by later generations.

When we'd ask about his childhood in the old country, he was apt to dismiss the question with the refrain "Did I ever tell you about two brothers with one pair of shoes?" That summed up his life in the old country.

Like other male adolescents, Dad was doomed to service in the Russian Army, a purgatory of hazings and beatings for young Jews. My grandfather Pesach, an ecclesiastical tailor, decreed that his firstborn son should do a vanishing act.

They put themselves in the hands of Ukrainian smugglers, who got them across the Polish border and on to Hamburg. There they boarded the SS *Kaiser Wilhelm der Grosse*, an immigrant ship, for a tipsy journey to New York. For the rest of his life my father could hardly look at a glass of water without getting seasick.

Already a skilled tailor, he went to work alongside his father in the sweatshops, the clothing factories, of lower Manhattan. My grandfather fell ill with an ailment the immigrant Jews called the sweets sickness. So casually diagnosed, this may or may not have been diabetes. After a tenement doctor failed him, he returned to Russia, convinced that old country medicine would save him. Within months he was dead.

As the oldest of five children, stranded in a foreign country, my father became the head of the family and its chief wage earner. He was still a teenager. With no schooling, unable to speak the language, he could nevertheless use a needle with quicker-than-the-eye dexterity. He survived. Scraping together steamboat fares, he brought over his mother, Celia, and his brothers and sisters.

The sweatshops, with their ten- and twelve-hour workdays, quickly lost their luster. Somewhere in his twenties Dad hung up his thimble.

By the time he met my mother, he was having a brief career in crime. He'd bought a taxicab.

The thievery was in the black meter that recorded the galloping fare. If the wheels hit a bump, the meter jumped a cent or two.

When my father discovered this mechanical windfall, he got to know every pothole in the streets of the city. The meter was empowering. If a passenger was rude or otherwise obnoxious, he got a very bumpy ride. To this day I cannot sit in a taxi without watching the meter for bumps.

He tired of this life of petty crime, for he soon sold the taxi. He'd come from a tradition of what village Jews called *luftmenshen*—men of air. That is to say, impractical dreamers who necessarily mastered a dozen trades to keep afloat. When not starving as tailors, my great-uncles were able to starve as rural violinists, clarinetists, and weekend bootleggers. On Saturday nights, when the state liquor shops were closed, they'd slip a pint of sacramental kosher wine to men from the Gentile side of the river (that side, by the way, called the village not Olik but Olyka).

Dad embraced the American Dream, a business of his own, and opened a notions and ribbon shop. It failed, but no matter. When I was almost two years old, he hopped a train for California in pursuit of his destiny. Within weeks he sent for my mother, my older sister, and me.

It has not escaped my notice that there is a certain family resemblance in the gallery of fathers and father proxies I have drawn in my novels. Most are birds of passage, airy optimists with nimble skills, each on a westward migration. Praiseworthy, the butler in *By the Great Horn Spoon!* runs off to the California gold rush (and strikes it rich when barbering miners' hair; he discovers gold dust in it). The magician-father in *Mr. Mysterious & Company* is heading for San Diego with his family to settle down at last. And Will Buckthorn, the grand rascal of *Chancy and the Grand Rascal*, describes himself as "a wayfaring printer, mule skinner, soldier, tinkerer, barn painter and everything in between." The grand rascal is the very picture of a Midwest *luftmensh*.

I can't say that I had had my father up front in my mind when I was writing these characters. But when I finished the novels and took a look, there he was.

SONNY BOY

I've loved your book Jingo Django.
Have you read it?

It was highly improbable that my mother's parents should ever have met. It could happen only because of the shifting about of European peoples, like tectonic plates, in the last century.

A red-bearded emigrant from somewhere in Russia washes up in Leeds, England, and sets up a small carpet slipper factory. The tops made from carpet remnants, these bedroom slippers were common even when I was a child.

Years later, in another tide of immigration, a beer-drinking, German-speaking young Jew from Lithuania embarks for America, where the streets are paved with gold. Having no sense of direction, he finds himself in Leeds and gets a temporary job in a carpet slipper factory. There he falls in love with the owner's sixteen-year-old daughter. And so Jerome Solomon marries Betsy Baker.

The steamship companies are having a furious rate war; for a couple of dollars each the newlyweds make the steerage voyage to New York. He becomes a vest presser. And there they begin to beget.

My mother, Sadie, was born. Nine more children followed, most of them girls, and I was provided with a galaxy of laughing, noisy, pretty, overweight, and loving aunts. They in turn produced a star shower of cousins.

My mother, a very bright girl, left school in the sixth grade. She was needed to help support the population explosion at home and went to work. A mere child, she operated a sewing machine in a factory making lady's shirtwaists (as blouses were then called). Laws outlawing child labor were far off in the future. She'd speak in whispers about the notorious Triangle Shirtwaist Company fire of 1911. It traumatized her. In a sweatshop building lacking sufficient exits, almost 150 young women and girls like herself were trapped and burned to death. It galvanized the union movement and led to improved working conditions. Once women were given the right to vote, my mother became a lifelong Democrat.

Grown into an attractive young women, she worked in a lady's hat shop. With an eye for bright, Gypsy colors, she walked into a nearby notions and ribbon store to find some trim for a hat. There she met a trim young man from Olik.

My sister Pearl was their firstborn. I came along a couple of years later, in Brooklyn, on March 16, 1920. I was given the Jewish name Avrom Zalmon. This my mother anglicized to Albert Sidney. At first I was called Sonny Boy until I got old enough to object, and then Sid. I was seven or eight years old before my mother thought I ought to know that my first name was Albert. It was shocking news to me. *Albert!* Sonny Boy had been bad enough. The name must have been a passing fancy that she'd cooled on. She apologized. I didn't care for

15

Pearl and I with Ma and Dad in Balboa Park. We had just arrived in San Diego the year before. Notice how people dressed up in those days for a Sunday in the park.

it, either, and still use it only on legal documents.

I have no early memories of Brooklyn or my grandfather, the presser of vests. He was run over by a soft-drink truck. I was two years old when my father sent us train tickets to join him among the palm trees in San Diego.

MODERN TIMES

I read Jim Ugly
instead of playing Nintendo.

One of my earliest memories is learning to button my own shoes. You slipped a small chrome hook through the button-hole in the leather, captured the ball-shaped button by the neck, and pulled it, strangling, through the eyelet.

I remember the feeling of triumph when I got the job done, button after button. But the need for this skill was fleeting, for the shoelace was becoming triumphant. I had to start all over again, learning to tie bows.

There were still horses pulling wagons on the streets then, in the mid-1920s, and rusting iron hitching posts lined the streets. But like shoe buttons, horses were becoming relics. Model T Fords zipped about everywhere, breeding like cockroaches. Modern times had arrived.

My father owned a black Maxwell with windows made of flexible isinglass, a sort of primitive clear plastic you snapped in place on cold nights or when it rained. Like other Jews, Dad reacted to Henry Ford's noisy and toxic anti-Semitism,

17

and for the rest of his life he refused to own a Ford—or even to ride in one.

I had my first driving lesson in the Maxwell. I was about five. Europeans like my father ate their main meals at noon, and he would drive home for my mother's home-cooked dishes. We lived then in a narrow wooden bungalow on the slope of Twenty-fifth Street, near the corner at J.

He'd crimp the front wheels against the downhill curb and set the hand brake. While he was enjoying his borscht, I climbed behind the steering wheel and pretended I was driving. Somehow I loosened the hand brake. Somehow I straightened the wheel.

I quickly noticed that scenery was traveling past the windows. I don't remember being frightened. I just remember concentrating my attention wonderfully on the golden oak steering wheel. I tried to crimp the front tires back against the curb, the way I'd seen it done.

A neighbor let out a yell, and my parents came flying out of the house. By then, by the friction of rubber against the curb, I'd got the Maxwell to stop near the corner. What was all the fuss about? I'd parked the car, hadn't I?

I wasn't punished. My father just looked at me with Svengali eyes, hypnotist's eyes, and said quietly, "Sonny, don't do that again."

I nodded even though I felt fully qualified for my driver's license.

In a way I punished myself sometime later when I got into some chocolate that turned out to be Ex-Lax. I remember my humiliation when Bubba, my silent grandmother from Olik, threw me onto some newspapers and cleaned me up. "*Feh!*" she burst out from time to time, calling forth the Yiddish expletive for anything unsavory. *"Feh!"* Those were two of not more than twenty words she addressed to me all the years I was growing up.

It doesn't rain in San Diego in the summer. J Street was not yet paved, and I remember watching the summer water truck creeping along with a peacock's tail of spray to hold down the yellowish red dust. Far more exciting was to hear the drone of a bumblebee high overhead. You'd look up and spot the stubby navy airplane, propeller-driven, practicing loops and rolls in the sky.

Although it had ended a few years before, World War I was still up front in the imaginations of boys my age. We

My parents hugging and mugging for the box camera, 1923.

19

romanticized everything from helmets and trenches—even the mud—to air battles. As early as the first grade I'd draw sleek Spads and Nieuports, our planes, in buzzing combat with the enemy, the checkered, villainous Fokkers. These German biplanes and triplanes we always drew curling vertically to earth, trailing scribbles of black, you-asked-for-it smoke.

With military bases a home industry, San Diego was a great place for parades. One I eagerly looked forward to came marching up Broadway each November 11, Armistice Day (Veterans Day, as it's now called). It was like a musical costume show, to the beat of great, thundering drums and trumpeting brasses. Here came the navy with bell-bottom trousers smartly tucked into white canvas leggings. At my ground level the footgear moved along like a parade of ducks.

The army marched by in chin-strapped helmets and highly polished Sam Browne belts. But soldiers looked like wallflowers at a party, for right behind came the peacocks of the parade, the U.S. Marines. Purplish black coats edged with fiery piping. Summer blue trousers with scarlet stripes running down the sides. The marines were in Technicolor before Technicolor was invented.

Generations overlap, and I didn't regard it as uncanny that I should watch Civil War veterans march by. They weren't arthritic ghosts. In campaign hats and with their chests ablaze with medals and ribbons, they were men in their eighties and nineties, and would march in many more parades.

My grammar school Spads and Fokkers had one more battle to fight in the windy skies over Europe. Grown up at last, I wrote a Warner Bros. film script about Americans during World War I who'd run off to fly in a special squadron for France. *Lafayette Escadrille* was meant to be an air epic on a scale with the ones I had drawn in school. It wasn't. I should have quit while I was ahead, in first grade.

In addition to shoelaces and the internal-combustion engine, another profound change had arrived in my pubescent life. Movies were beginning to talk out loud. I was totally baffled when I saw my first sound pictures. There was only one way I could figure out how it was done. People *must* be hidden behind the screen, talking through megaphones.

Finally there came to our house the marvel of them all, that great incomprehensible, the radio. Here I was soon to discover a daily serial sponsored by White King soap, *Chandu the Magician.*

It came on the air just before dinner, and I'd rush in from play to fling myself down alone before the family radio. On a spooky shimmer of sound, Chandu would transport himself in seconds to anywhere in the world where trouble beckoned. The great villains of London and Cairo and Hong Kong didn't stand a chance against Chandu's magic. I listened in worshipful, cathedral silence.

I vividly recall hurrying home just in time for Chandu when my mother spun the dial back to the station she'd been listening to and told me to leave the radio alone. Some new singer was singing, and she wanted to listen.

I was deeply frustrated. I didn't understand how anyone would rather listen to Bing Crosby than tune in to Chandu. I still don't.

6

ON MY WAY, BUT WHERE?

I read The Ghost in the Noonday Sun. *Keep your day job.*

My younger sister was almost born in Tijuana, Mexico, which was then a sort of Las Vegas of the Far West. Selling strong drink was against the law in the United States at that time, and so was gambling. Both were legal in Tijuana. The main street of this small, dusty border town was lined on both sides with beer joints and hole-in-the-wall twenty-four-hour nightclubs, each with slot machines along the walls. The sidewalks were open bazaars of tourist goods: earth brown pottery, live puppies, Mexican sandals, green and blue glassware, and a local folk art, straw donkeys. These foot-tall animals were handwoven and stiffly ridden by a man wearing a sombrero and a serape—hat and Mexican blanket thrown over the shoulder. These commonplace straw donkeys later were to play a role in launching my career as a novelist.

We were enjoying a Sunday picnic in a shady Tijuana park when my mother decided to have a baby. Dad threw Pearl and me in the car and raced to cross the border back into the

United States. He had to stop at the gate to flash his citizenship papers. The guards took a look at my mother and waved us across. Dad managed to reach a San Diego hospital, and Arlene was born, soon to be given the lifelong nickname Honey. It was Mother's Day. Our family was now complete.

It was about this time that someone else entered my life: Robin Hood. In earlier years my mother had sometimes read to Pearl and me; I vividly remember *Uncle Tom's Cabin.* My hatred for Simon Legree was fierce. I was glad to live safely in modern times when such meanness and cruelty wouldn't be allowed. I didn't know that in the wings waited Adolf Hitler and the other gargoyles of World War II.

One day I noticed a family friend, Danny Freeman, then in the fourth grade, sitting at the dining room table and casually reading the newspaper. I was hugely impressed. Wow! I became aware of my first ambition in life. I yearned to be able to read a newspaper.

In this regard a tremendous trifle occurred when I was in second grade at Sherman School. My turn came along to read aloud a simple paragraph in our schoolbook. With growing sharpness, the teacher corrected every word as it came rushing out of my mouth. I couldn't even get "the" and "and" right. My classmates began to titter. I turned crimson with humiliation. I wanted to shut the book and never read again.

It took me ages to figure out what had gone so wrong. Clearly I'd been reading the wrong paragraph. Why hadn't she caught on at once and spared me the wound?

I left my disgrace behind when we moved to a bungalow at Thirtieth and Juniper, and I transferred to Brooklyn Grammar School. It was a few yards from home, in front of the Piggly Wiggly grocery store, that I first entered the newspaper business. I hawked three-cent copies of the *San Diego Sun*. It was my first job.

When I was able to read the newspaper for myself, I didn't realize that something profound had happened to me. But books were no longer room furnishings, like lampshades. I was soon turning the pages of *Robin Hood* and could hear voices. I didn't need audio. I could hear the sharp clash of swords and pikestaffs.

I took up residence in Sherwood Forest for a solid year or two, and the experience has never entirely left me. I still can't pass up a discarded wood lath lying in the alley without thinking I could make a splintery sword out of it. And for years I recycled sticks and grocery string into bows and arrows. I crawled inside the Howard Pyle illustrations, and if I hadn't got hungry from time to time, I'd never have returned to San Diego with its noon whistle and its asphalt streets.

By the time I reached Roosevelt Junior High, I would have been designated a reluctant reader. But I was reading all of the time. I haunted the used-books shops on upper Broadway, looking for tomes on conjuring. I'd hop streetcars to scour the library branches. Magic books! I was reluctant to read anything else.

As a result, I didn't have time for Tom Swift or the Hardy Boys. I missed out on most of the wonderful junk reading.

I had my nose in shabby copies of such English classics as Professor Hoffmann's *Modern Magic* and Maskelyne and Devant's *Our Magic*. Not a hint of a plot in any of these hundreds of pages, but I hung in there. I was learning how to make a playing card float in the air. I found out how Harry Snyder had been able to run swords into a box, with Wanda inside, without butchering her.

Without realizing it, I was also absorbing a sense of language

24

and style from these Victorian masters—I enjoy reading them still—for they are to the literature of magic what Macaulay is to the writing of history.

But my constant companion was a shady and mysterious character, possibly a murderer, who around the turn of the century wrote an exposé of gambler's and magician's sleights called *The Expert at the Card Table*. He chose to sign himself S. W. Erdnase, an easily deciphered pseudonym. It's E. S. Andrews spelled backward.

Like so many magicians of this century, I learned sleight of hand from Erdnase's 1902 treatise, the sacred text of card magic. But to slog through the detailed and weedy instructions, you had to be driven. Here's a sample of vintage Erdnase, explaining how to palm off a selected card from the center of the pack:

"Now bring the right hand over deck with the little finger at side corner of protruding card, second and third fingers at middle of end, and first finger close to end corner, and the thumb close to the inner end corner of the deck. Apparently push the card straight home, but really push the protruding end with the right little finger. . . ."

It was about like trying to learn ballet off the printed page. I deciphered and learned the sleight he's describing, but in all the years since I have never had occasion to use it. I can still do the thing, just in case. What's unseen is quite pretty.

I kept my few props in a shoe box. One day I came home from school and the box was gone. Where was my handkerchief vanisher? Where were my deck of cards, my topsy-turvy match, my coin with a hook on it?

There was no one home. Had we been robbed? Where was my mother? Had my sister Pearl done this?

I made a wild search. I quickly discovered my shoe box and couple of paperback magic books in the backyard trash barrel, neatly balanced on top. It was almost as if a trail of breadcrumbs had been left for me to follow.

I rescued everything, and as soon as my mother returned with Honey, I shot her an injured but fiery look.

"Ma! Did you throw out my magic?"

She seemed pained and embarrassed. "Dad said you're too serious about this magic stuff. He said to get it out of the house and out of your system."

"It's not hurting anyone!"

"Dad says you'll starve."

"Houdini didn't starve!"

"Don't Houdini me."

I got the message. Dad wanted me warned. I kept my magic out of his sight for a while. Today I realize that he was right. If my son, Paul, had shown early signs of wanting to pull rabbits out of hats, I would have worried.

Most magicians *do* starve.

7
MY LIFE WITH THE TREBLE CLEF, SORT OF

The Whipping Boy is one of those kinds of books that you want to finish, yet you don't want it to end.

One day my dad came home with a clarinet, a folding music stand, and the notion that I might one day play Carnegie Hall.

I was never given a choice of instruments. Would I rather play the trombone or the harmonica?

"Schlemiel!" he said. "Nobody plays the trombone at weddings and bar mitzvahs. The harmonica—*feh!"* Clearly I was to become a *luftmensh* in training.

My mother found a music teacher, a slight and balding man named Mr. Gay, and I faced my first pages of black lines and little black notes. It was hate at first sight. I knew instantly that I'd never be able to read that crazy stuff. My brain froze at the thought.

In addition to his private students, Mr. Gay taught the school orchestra at junior high, and he installed me in the woodwind section.

The only note I could recognize with certainty was middle C. Nevertheless, I played in school orchestras all the way through my senior year in high school.

How did I get away with this musical hanky-panky? Simple—I learned to play by ear. At rehearsal, if the clarinet beside me went up, I went up. Down, and I went down. Rest, and I rested.

I'd have the piece of music memorized by the end of the first rehearsal. It would have been a thousand times easier to learn to read the music. But I had a fixed and absolute notion that I *couldn't* learn it. I wouldn't try. Decades later, when I decided I wanted to learn to play the classical guitar, I sat down and learned to read music. *Schlemiel!* It was simple.

And I came close to playing Carnegie Hall at that. Many years later I was informed that a novel of mine, *Humbug Mountain,* was a finalist in the National Book Awards. I was asked to write and send along an acceptance speech *in advance,* with the ceremonies to take place in the famous concert hall.

It seemed a cruel request; what if one didn't win? But they needed the advance text for the printer in the event one did, so I delivered a text. The lead sentence came to me at once.

"When I was kid," I wrote, "my father stuck a clarinet in my hand and said that one day I'd play Carnegie Hall. I'm delighted to have made it, at last."

I didn't win the award.

PALS

How did you survive junior high?

It was by mere chance that I noticed in the newspaper a filler about a club meeting coming up in North Park. Not a mere gathering of Rotarians or Elks or Moose. *Wizards!* The paper announced that the next meeting of the San Diego Magicians Club would convene in a real estate office at Thirty-second and University.

I'd never imagined such a group existed. And North Park was only a short streetcar ride away.

I was a shy fourteen-year-old, and I can't now imagine how I got up the courage to search out the place. But I loaded up my pockets with a couple of magic props, and one hot August morning I headed for North Park.

I found the real estate office easily enough. Through the narrow window I saw an imposing white-haired man as he turned in his swivel chair to spit in a spittoon. Then he replaced the cigar in his mouth and returned to some papers on a large rolltop desk. Was this a magician?

I couldn't keep standing there: he was beginning to notice

me out of the corners of his gray eyes. I took a breath, entered, and met Professor Fait the Great.

"Sir, can I come in?"

"You're in." Not unfriendly.

"Is this where the magicians meet?"

"Are you a magician?" Not a snicker. Straightforward.

"I can do some thimble sleights. And some other stuff."

"Let me see." Not patronizing. Man to man.

I put a thimble on the tip of my index finger. I made it disappear and reappear. I made it jump from one finger to the other. As he watched, he began sticking three silver dollars to the August sweat on his forehead.

He gave an acknowledging nod when I finished with the thimble and asked, "Which coin: left, middle, or right?"

"Middle," I said.

The middle coin fell from his forehead. Then, on command, the left and right without the slightest shimmy of the skin. I didn't think it was much of a trick, but he burst into a triumphant smile. It was his trademark feat, and I was to see him do it hundreds of times in the years ahead. He was the president of the magic club, Charles W. Fait.

"What else can you do?" he asked.

I took out a coin of my own and made it vanish, using the French Drop, a classic sleight. "Is there any chance I can join the magic club?"

"None," he said, turning to the spittoon once more. "We don't have any boys in the club."

"Oh."

A shift of the eyes. "But I'll see what I can do. Now, you're doing the French Drop too fast. Take your time. What's your name? Sidney? Slow down, Sidney. And remember that peo-

HOKUS-POKUS AT ELECTRICAL EXPO

The Magicians' club of San Diego is treating crowds at the free Electrical exposition, Broadway pier, to some "now you see it—now you don't" entertainment. Above (left to right) are Sidney Fleischman; Thomas Bannan, ventriloquist, and Buddy Ryan. C. W. Fait (below) holds dollars on his face by muscular action and drops any one designated at will.

Professor Fait doing his coin-on-the-face trick. In the background Buddy Ryan is producing silk handkerchiefs from a canister. I am showing off the billiard ball trick in one hand and card fans in the other. The only one who doesn't look wooden is the dummy.

ple look where you look, so let your eyes follow your empty fist as if the coin were really in there. Try it again. And what's your phone number? I'll talk to a couple of the boys and let you know."

Before I left, he dug through a drawer and handed me one of his old handbills and a newspaper clipping. He'd been a small-town magician, traveling for thirty-three years throughout the Midwest with his own full evening show. He'd retired from the footlights, like a lot of other show people, to the sunshine of San Diego, and opened a real estate office.

A couple of nights later my sister Pearl called me to the phone. "*Sidney*, it's for you." At last someone in the family realized that I'd outgrown Sonny.

I heard Professor Fait's voice. "We'll let you join the club," he said. "Can you scrape up the dues? It's a dollar a year."

"I'll be in tomorrow," I said, my heart sounding like a

This card was my passport through adolescence.

drop hammer. I felt the need to act fast, before the magicians changed their minds.

After accepting my dues, Professor Fait recovered a letter from one of the dark caverns in his desk and handed it to me. The newspaper item had flagged the attention of another youngling. His name was Buddy Ryan, he was fifteen, and he had just moved to San Diego from Whitefish, Montana. Could he have details on joining the magic club?

"Why don't you look him up and let us know what you think?"

Suddenly not only was I a club member, but I was given an oar to pull.

The boy from Whitefish lived only a few blocks from me, in a gray wooden bungalow on Granada Avenue. I knocked, and when the door opened, I met the kid who was to become my best friend and adventurer in magic for almost forty years.

"Are you Buddy Ryan?"

"Yup."

I announced with a heavy air of self-importance that I was from the San Diego Magicians Club. He seemed impressed. "What sort of magic do you do?" I asked.

He showed me. He had a large chest of the most amazing props I'd ever seen. He had a Sucker Die Box and a top hat. He showed me a Welsh Rarebit Pan and a magician's velvet table with a hidden pocket in it—equipment I'd seen illustrated in the pages of Professor Hoffmann's book. I couldn't have been in greater awe had I stumbled on to King Solomon's mine.

"Where did you get all this stuff?" I asked.

"From Ajax the Great."

"Who's he?"

"Some magician in Detroit who was quitting and selling all his stuff."

"How much?" A million?

"Ten dollars," Buddy said, and pulled a pack of Wings cigarettes out of his pocket. He smoked.

In those Depression days a loaf of bread was nine cents. Ten dollars was serious money. Had the opportunity come my way, I wouldn't have been able to raise so vast a sum. Buddy's father, before his recent death, had been an engineer on the Great Northern Railway and had had an assured income. So it was that Ajax the Great found someone to buy his props and vanished from the world of magic.

With a shy, tentative smile Buddy asked, "What sort of magic do you do?"

 In those days I would no more leave home without a thimble and a deck of cards in my pocket than I'd venture forth without my streetcar pass. I made a card disappear by back-palming it out of sight behind my fingers. "I've seen that in the books," Buddy said. But he hadn't mastered it.

He'd never before seen thimble magic. When I finished, he was clearly stunned and fooled. We became instant pals and conspirators. The differences between us were congenial. In those days, with a bit of funding, one could go into box magic, as Buddy had. Without dollars for props, one was apt to go into sleight of hand, as I had.

We lived in each other's houses, making plans to give shows for handsome fees. We'd try things on Pearl and especially Honey, who was then an indulgent seven-year-old, eager to applaud us.

Then we'd practice our notions on Buddy's older sister, Mary, who one day became our slim, smiling magicians' assistant, and his widowed mother. Mrs. Ryan, suffering terribly from asthma, had packed up her two teenage kids and left the harsh winters of Whitefish. Thin and drawn, she hoped her health would improve in the benign San Diego climate.

Mrs. Ryan typed a lot on a noisy portable. And I'd begun to notice a magazine that she seemed to read from cover to cover every month. Something called the *Writer's Digest*.

I didn't know that average people could be writers. I thought you had to be a genius, born with a quill pen in your hand. I began to flip through the magazine. There were articles on how to write dialogue and how to create story characters that live.

It was my first peek into the world of the aspiring writer next door, like Mrs. Ryan. I wasn't interested.

THE MIRTHFUL CONJURERS

---

*In case you ever need an actress
I'll always be available.*

The most important night of the month for Buddy and me came on the third Monday, at seven-thirty, when the magic club assembled. We were almost always the first ones to turn up at Professor Fait's real estate office. We'd be expected to perform some trick or new skill, like everyone else. No quarter was given because we were kids. We'd prepare as carefully and nervously as if each occasion were a Broadway opening.

The membership was a patchwork of men. His hands permanently tattooed with grease, Eddy Goodwin was a bicycle mechanic. Benjamin O. Lacy taught physics at San Diego High School. There was a retired ventriloquist, a watchmaker, a naturopath doctor who drove one of the miniature Austins, hardly larger than a wind-up toy, that had begun to appear on the streets.

I was thrilled to discover that Harry Snyder, that demigod in bow tie and spats, had been a member. Eddy Goodwin knew him well and said he was doing WPA shows in the Los

Angeles area. The Works Progress Administration had put a lot of actors, writers, and showpeople to work.

Within a few months Buddy and I felt quite at home in the company of magicians, and joining skills, we eagerly put together our own forty-five-minute show. We called ourselves the Mirthful Conjurers. Our wit came largely from boilerplate patter supplied with the instruction sheets. I remember my saucy opening remark: "There's nothing up my sleeves but my arms." That's how mirthful we were.

But we did succeed in booking ourselves around town. With suitcases full of props, we hopped streetcars to our engagements. We produced silk handkerchiefs from painted metal tubes. Buddy cut a rope in two and restored it, at that time a brand-new effect. By then I was able to do the multiplying

A GLITTERING ARRAY OF MYSTERIES

BUDDY RYAN
AND
SIDNEY FLEISCHMAN

"THE MIRTHFUL CONJURERS"

PHONE: H-7430   4376 FLORIDA ST.
—H-8379-R   3557 RAY ST.

Buddy was fifteen, I was fourteen, when we declared ourselves to be professional magicians and had these business cards printed up. Our adjectives were more theatrical than literal.

MAGIC **COMING!** MYSTERY

BUD & SID

R Y A N

PRESENT

SEE'N IS BELIEV'N

CAN!

AN EXAMINED BULLET BE SHOT THRU A HUMAN BODY
Yet Cause NO Wound ? ?

THE GREAT EAST INDIAN ROPE TRICK BE PRODUCED ? ?

AN ORDINARY CANE FLOAT AND DO TRICKS IN MID-AIR ? ?

THE SPIRITS RETURN ? ?

MANY OTHER IMPOSSIBILITIES TAKE PLACE ? ?

YOU WILL ANSWER

YES!!

AFTER WITNESSING

SEE'N IS BELIEV'N

PLAYING

"A Glittering Array Of Mysteries"

I ran off thousands of these handbills in high school print shop. We'd tack them to telephone poles and fences to announce the arrival of our summer show of wonders. Magicians have been killed doing bullet tricks, but the one we did was quite safe.

billiard ball trick I'd first seen in the hands of Harry Snyder. Our fee was $2.50 for the full forty-five minute extravaganza. That didn't put us on easy street, but close enough.

And then calamity. Mary was transferring to the University of California at Berkeley, and the family moved to Northern California. One day Buddy was gone.

A grandiose scheme arose in the exchange of letters that followed. Why not take a show of our own "on the road" next summer? Wasn't that every magic kid's ambition, to tour with his own show?

Our letters began to run from ten to twenty pages as we laid plans. We decided to call our show *See'n Is Believ'n*. Buddy, with a mechanical bent, would take woodshop and build some of the props we lacked. I would take printshop and run off handbills and tickets we'd need. Toward the end of spring the shop teacher complained that I had half the school type tied up in my projects. I managed to run off thousands of broadsides before he made me distribute the type.

Meanwhile, Mrs. Ryan offered to help buy a car for our travels, as long as we could find one for less than fifty dollars. We needed after-school jobs, in addition to what shows we were able to turn up solo. I got a job in a grocery store a couple of blocks from Professor Fait's real estate office.

One day I was stocking shelves when Bubba, my silent, unsmiling grandmother from Olik, walked in. Even though it had been decades since she'd left the old country, she still dressed like a peasant in a heavy ankle-length skirt and a scarf around her toast brown hair. Her face brightened when she saw me. I didn't know she could smile. And then she began to talk to me. In *English*.

I was astonished. When had she learned to speak English? Why had she kept it a secret?

She bought a box of candles, said good-bye, smiled, and left. I never saw her alive again.

Buddy and I team up as the Mirthful Conjurers. Evidently Buddy with the wand in his hand has just turned a live rabbit into a stuffed one.

McBROOM

---

*If that McBroom story
is true, I'm stupid.*

We had moved to North Park, and I thought nothing of walking in on Professor Fait anytime I was free. He seemed glad to pass an hour or so telling stories, mostly about his adventures as a small-town showman. With the Depression at its meanest, the real estate business was largely a fantasy. He had plenty of time, had grown a bit lame, and loved to sit in his swivel chair and talk.

He slapped silver dollars on his forehead and said, "Did I tell you about the time up in Minnesota, out at Blackduck Lake, when a fellow bet me eight dollars and fifty cents cash that I couldn't row his birchbark canoe out to the island without capsizing? Left, right, or middle?"

"Left."

The chosen coin fell from his forehead. "Well, I'd never seen a canoe I couldn't ride and slapped down the cash. When I sat myself in the canoe, I found at once it was so finely balanced that it threw me like a wild mustang. You'd think the bottom was buttered. But I realized quick enough what

41

was wrong. I had two silver dollars in my pocket, my right pocket, and that was throwing the balance off. So I shifted one of those dollars to my left pocket, picked up the oar again, and prepared to set out for the island. But that infernal canoe threw me again."

His forehead shed the middle coin.

"Well, that fellow—his name was Jenkins, Amos T. Jenkins—he was laughing and picking up the winnings when I saw my face in the water and detected what was throwing me off-balance. 'You ain't won yet, Mr. Jenkins,' I told him, and got out my silver pocket comb. I'd parted my hair on the right, Sidney, and it was enough to throw the birchbark canoe off-balance. I cut a fresh part in my hair, straight down the center of my head—and rode out to the island smooth as a duck.''

No flash of a smile. His delivery had been straight-faced and conversational, as if to guarantee the amazing truthfulness of what had happened. I'd never heard a tall tale before, and I didn't know what to make of it. Did he expect me to believe this? Was he slightly addled? Would he be insulted if I laughed?

I called out the final coin remaining on his forehead. He let it fall—and burst out laughing. That gave me permission, and I laughed, too.

I couldn't have guessed how important these moments would be when the tall tale and I again crossed paths. That broad European humor had emigrated, taken out citizenship papers, and become thoroughly Americanized around the cracker barrel. It was moribund by the 1960s, when I was reminded of Professor Fait's canoe story and began to research this richly inventive and folkloric form of comedy. Before long a character named Josh McBroom leaped out of my typewriter,

Madame Houdini, the great escape artist's widow, autographs a playing card for me. I came to know her in the mid-1930s, when she retired to Southern California after Houdini's death. Full of encouragement, she was a kind of den mother to us young West Coast magicians.

together with his amazing one-acre prairie farm, his wife, and eleven children. The topsoil was so rich he could grow two or three crops a *day*. Pumpkins shot up so fast that the kids hopped on them for rides. If you dropped a nickel on that one-acre farm, it would grow to a quarter before you could bend and pick it up.

Until McBroom came along, the tall tale had been entirely anecdotal and episodic. I gave the stories architecture, with beginnings, middles, and ends. Over the years I was to write ten books about McBroom; I retreaded Professor Fait's canoe story in *McBroom's Almanac*.

If my father had became resigned to my crazy show business aspirations, he gave no sign of it until the San Diego Magicians Club threw a picnic one Sunday and he turned up with my mother. He couldn't have been more genial and friendly to Professor Fait and the others. I overheard my colleagues praise my skill, and I think Dad saw at once that magicians were as obsessed as mad poets. If he left me alone, maybe I'd get over it.

11

SEE'N IS BELIEV'N

---

*Please don't come back to my school.
I hate to write letters.*

It was 1936. By the time school let out for the summer, I had two suitcases packed with magic gimmicks and a toothbrush. I caught the SS *Yale* for an overnight boat trip up the coast to San Francisco, where Buddy was waiting on the dock.

We found a boxy, dark green 1928 Essex for thirty-five dollars. After a couple of weeks of rehearsal in Berkeley, we stuffed the back of the car like a turkey with show props. There were trick boxes Buddy had made, cardboard boxes packed with *See'n Is Believ'n* handbills, silk handkerchiefs, two magic tables, ropes, a large canvas mail sack, sleeping bags, our dress-up suits—eleven suitcases in all, not including a live white rat in a cage we needed for a comedy trick. We'd invite several people onstage, pour them free drinks from a black bottle, then break the glass and show the white rat inside. We promised mirth, didn't we?

Buddy's sister, Mary, had written a number of letters in an attempt to book our show in advance, but the only favorable reply she received came from the Emerald Bay Camp and

Hotel on the western edge of Lake Tahoe. Yes, wrote Mr. Salter, we could perform there on the Friday night of July 10.

And so we set out for the Sierra Nevada Mountains to the east, our hearts singing, our destination as fixed as the North Star. Buddy drove, Mary sat between us, and her German shepherd, Pal, rode behind the luggage carrier on the running board, his tongue hanging out all the way.

We passed a sign posted on a crossroads tree, pointing the way to a CCC camp deep in the woods. Buddy stepped on the brakes, backed up, and we looked at the sign again. Everyone in those days knew what the CCC was: the Civilian Conservation Corps. The Roosevelt administration had set up camps in

The oil-gulping 1928 Essex we bought for thirty-five dollars to go touring with our magic show. The German shepherd on the running board was Pal, who went "on the road" with us.

the foothills and mountains to provide healthy outdoor work for unemployed teenagers and young men. Dressed in U.S. Army clothing, they cleared underbrush, put in fire roads, and built bridges. Maybe they needed some entertainment.

We followed the dirt road through a couple of miles of pine trees and discovered our financial life preserver. The commanding officer welcomed a morale booster and gladly agreed to our five-dollar fee. Following dinner we put on our hour-and-a half "Glittering Array of Mysteries." After that we never passed up a CCC sign, and we were never turned away.

It was my first performance under the name Sid Ryan. In setting up our handbill, I found that my long name added clutter to clutter. We decided to pass ourselves off as brothers.

But I don't think anyone was fooled. We both were dark-haired and brown-eyed, but Buddy's complexion was as mushroom white as if he'd just ventured forth from a Montana winter. If I passed under a fifteen-watt lightbulb, I got a nice tan. He didn't look Jewish. I didn't look Irish. But the Ryan brothers we were. That's show biz.

We packed up the Essex and continued on our way, climbing ever higher into the Sierras. I would never have imagined that there lay in wait for me story material I would turn into two novels, *Jim Ugly* and *By the Great Horn Spoon!*

In El Dorado County, Kyburz Lodge let us put on a floor show for its Saturday night dance and pass the hat. We collected over eight dollars!

But good fortune doesn't smile forever. The Thursday before we were due in Lake Tahoe, the Essex let out a loud, banging clatter as if the engine were chewing up nuts and bolts and shooting them out the exhaust. We discovered a clutch of rustic tourist cabins around the next bend and tried to push the heavily loaded car uphill. With all of us shoving, we advanced about an eighth of an inch.

Buddy announced with some certainty that we had thrown a tie rod. Where were we going to get a replacement for a 1928 Essex tie rod way up here in the mountains? How were we going to get our show to Emerald Bay for our big Friday night engagement? Tomorrow!

Buddy started up the car and defiantly drove it, clanging and jangling, the half mile to the tourist outpost of civilization. We rented a cabin (thank you, Kyburz!), and Buddy crawled under the car with a handful of wrenches. He drained the oil and removed the oil pan. Yes, it was a tie rod.

The owner of the cabins, a sparrowlike graying woman, gave us the number of a garage in Sacramento in the valley below. Hallelujah! They had the part and would send it up with the milk truck the following morning.

We paid for the tie rod on arrival, and Buddy, who seemed confident that he knew what he was doing, took out the old rod and installed the new one. Since the Essex burned a lot of oil, we'd carried a five-gallon can with us from Berkeley. Buddy reappeared from under the car and began pouring oil back into the spout. Mary and I stood watching, ready to hit the road for Emerald Bay. It was getting late.

"Boy, this car holds a lot of oil," Buddy said as he tipped the can to empty it.

Suddenly Mary jumped back. She was standing in oil. We all were standing in oil. Buddy broke into a sudden, sheepish grin. He'd installed the tie rod perfectly. But he'd forgot to replace the oil plug, and our supply of oil had poured through the car as easily as a funnel.

While the car was now fixed, we had no oil. The lady of

the cabins thought she had a couple of cans in the cobwebs somewhere. When we pulled back onto the highway, we were reduced to pennies.

We coasted down the steep cliff road to Emerald Bay at a little after six-thirty, with the after-dinner show to start at eight. The trouble was it took us two hours to unpack and set up the show, suitcase by suitcase.

We took moments to shower, for Mr. Salter, the proprietor, kindly provided us with accommodations. We ate while hurriedly putting the show together. The larger props were made to break down for packing, so there were endless screws and latches and wing bolts to deal with. Silk handkerchiefs had to be loaded into their secret compartments. White powder had to be mixed with water to look like milk for the vanishing milk trick. A thousand details.

The recreation hall began to fill up. Mountain residents were coming down out of the pines to see the live show. Eight o'clock came and went. We had a full house. But at eight-thirty we still weren't ready. I went out in front of the curtain and explained about our car trouble. To vamp for time, I did a talkative card trick in which I counted six cards, threw away three, but still had six cards. I tossed away another three. I still showed six. And once more. And again. It's a trick I still perform.

Finally we opened the show, continuing to unpack on the sly as we went along. It was a most amiable audience, and we heard cheers when we finished. Buddy was seventeen. I was sixteen. We regarded it as a triumph. Mr. Salter even wrote the Ryan brothers a letter of recommendation.

TRUCKEE

*Now I'm going to tell you
about my summer vacation.*

Where to? Once the Essex climbed back up the cliff road from Emerald Bay, we had no fixed destination. We wandered aimlessly along the roads, foraging for show dates. We climbed higher into the mountains until we reached the big city of the Sierras, Truckee. It had a couple of streets and a movie house, the Magnolia.

We found the cowboy-booted manager sweeping the place out. We showed him our letter of recommendation from Mr. Salter, but it cut no ice with him. He turned us away and went on sweeping. I was eventually able to find a sublime way to "play" that theater. In the novel *Jim Ugly* my fictional drama company opens its show at the Magnolia, and the theater becomes one of the principal story locations.

We learned that an upstairs Masonic hall could be rented. We made arrangements to give the lodge 20 percent of the box-office receipts; the show would go on the following night. We papered the telephone poles with our handbills. In the doorway we put up a lobby display sign we'd had painted in Berkeley; a dog promptly came along and anointed one of our photographs.

I'd learned in school about the notorious Donner Party, who'd been snowbound during the last century and resorted to cannibalism. We were there. Truckee hadn't existed then, but this is where it happened. Here among these dark pines covering the hills as thickly as wolf's fur. As we hung around town, my sense of living history was launched.

We performed our hour-and-a-half show to a paying audience of fewer than two dozen people. From an old letter home, I see that our box-office receipts amounted to $5.95. The Masonic lodge shrugged and accepted its $1.19 share for the use of the hall, and we moved on.

I left Truckee with a lingering memory of place. That night Pal, Mary's dog, got into a fight with a skunk. It took him a week crouched like a pariah on the running board to air out. That, too, got into the Truckee novel, but in altered form.

I had never owned a dog and became immensely fond of Pal. All summer long he was mine, but he wasn't mine. Jake Bannock in the novel inherits his father's one-man dog, Jim Ugly—his, but not his. While the story starts on the Nevada flats where Jake puts the dog, with his keen nose, on the trail of the boy's vanished actor father, events quickly move up the Sierras to Truckee.

Art is presto chango. While Pal was my model for the novel, he became half wolf, arrogant and inscrutable. The *See'n Is Believ'n* troupe was transformed into an itinerant company of dramatic actors. Wanda of the ten-in-one show changed into the sharpshooting Arizona Girl performing a three-act feminist

51

drama, *Mrs. William Tell* (it is really she, behind a tree, who shoots the apple off their son's head). When the boy actor playing William Tell's son is blasted by a skunk in the Truckee woods, Jake replaces him and continues on with the company.

Presto chango.

GOLD FEVER

*I think people shouldn't go
through life without reading
By the Great Horn Spoon!*

We came down with gold fever. We'd been in and out of old gold rush towns such as Hangtown and Rough and Ready, but it was only when we'd wandered far north to summer-baked Weaverville that visions of yellow nuggets danced in our heads.

There the manager of the movie theater agreed to book us. A man in shirtsleeves and suspenders, he seemed as smitten with Mary as with our show. He kept offering her drinks from his pint bottle of bourbon.

He mentioned in passing that when local kids needed to scrape up theater money, they panned gold dust out of their front yards. We immediately bought gold pans.

We'd have to hang around Weaverville for three days, providing the manager time to mail our handbills to nearby hamlets and otherwise promote the show. Three days would give us plenty of time to strike it rich.

Along one of the streams we found a friendly and talkative old prospector named Rosey, with a floppy hat and a sweeping

53

mustache, who taught us how to manipulate our gold pans.

We scuttled like crabs along the stream banks. Mary came along, dodging the theater manager, and wrote letters home in the shade. Rosey had told us that gold dust and flakes were apt to get tangled in the roots of weeds.

"Wash out the roots in your pans, boys," he said.

After three days the stream banks looked as neat as a Bel Air estate; we'd plucked every weed. We didn't find the merest flake of "color," as us prospectors learned to call it. But I came away with a strong sense of romance about the old gold rush diggings.

I was to strike a mother lode after all. Many who are familiar with my work will recognize here the first stirrings of the widely read gold rush novel *By the Great Horn Spoon!* Never out of print since it was published in 1963, it was made into a Disney film (as *Bullwhip Griffin*, don't ask me why) and has been translated around the world. The bit about the weeds turned up in Chapter Eleven.

People around Weaverville must have been starved for entertainment, for almost every theater seat was filled on the blast-furnace night of the performance. The manager kept wetting down the sidewalk and entry with a garden hose in a primitive version of air conditioning.

Not only was Mary our "box jumper" (the assistant in magic shows who jumps into magic boxes and vanishes or is sawed in half), but she did a novelty turn of her own: rag pictures.

Creating pictures with rags was a minor vaudeville art, now vanished. The easel was covered with black felt. Mary would lay on oddly shaped pieces of colored felt that easily clung. Finally she stepped back to display a Hawaiian scene with

I pan for gold. Buddy and I together didn't find enough to fill the smallest tooth cavity. The homemade sluice box belonged to our mentor, Rosey. Gold flakes and nuggets, being heavy, would get trapped in the rough bottom as dirt was sluiced through the box. In my gold rush novel *By the Great Horn Spoon!* I call one chapter "The Man in the Jipijapa Hat." Here I'm wearing a jipijapa hat. When seagoing forty-niners reached Panama, they discovered wonderfully flexible straw hats from Jipijapa, Ecuador. In time they began referring to the headgear as panama hats. I figured today's kids reading the book wouldn't know what a panama hat was, so I opted for the original name, with its marvelous look and especially for its jolly sound.

palm trees and a full tropical moon shining on the ocean. Applause!

I was backstage, meanwhile, reaching into the rat's cage to load him into the compartment for the bottle trick. He didn't want to be disturbed and sank his teeth into my thumb. I managed to catch and load him. We'd been assured by an expert at the pet shop in Berkeley that he was male. No wonder the rat bit me. The next morning we discovered several pink newborns in the cage.

To escape the heat, we headed west to the ocean and by the end of summer returned triumphant to Berkeley. By that time we'd had so many blowouts, our tires looked like patched underwear. There were no spoils to divide up, but we'd brought to life our adolescent fantasy of taking a show on the road.

With great prescience, my mother had sent me five dollars from her poker winnings to make sure I had bus fare home. Mary returned to the university and Buddy to Berkeley High. I settled in at San Diego High, where I was about to bump into Petruchio. 1936—O joyous year!

17

TRANSFORMATIONS

I despise reading, but
The Whipping Boy *is a book*
I could not stop reading.

My remaining years at San Diego High School, on a breezy hilltop overlooking downtown and the harbor, would hardly need mentioning except for a class that transformed my scholarly life.

By chance I found myself in an English class conducted by Harry Jones, a heavyset, sharp-nosed, no-nonsense but gifted teacher. He didn't believe that Shakespeare should be read; the plays should be acted out. And so we were assigned parts, and I was to be a character whose name I couldn't even pronounce—Petruchio.

Every day we sat at our desks, performing our way through *The Taming of the Shrew*. Once we got the hang of the language and the drift of the story, we began to have the fun of our lives.

By great good fortune, a replica of the original Globe Theatre had been built for the San Diego World's Fair in Balboa Park. While I had in the past avoided the ye olde place in favor of midway attractions, I now ventured inside and sat through a performance of *The Comedy of Errors*. I was spellbound. The world might already know that Shakespeare was great, but I was just finding it out.

I began to haunt the place. And for the first time I began to read something other than magic books. Ambling through school, I was leaving behind a history of C scholarship. Suddenly I turned into an A student.

Mr. Jones seemed faintly angry that I wasn't entertaining thoughts of going to college. The thought had never occurred to me. I'd be the first male Fleischman to graduate from high school. Wasn't that achievement enough? And college was expensive, wasn't it?

With the Depression ever deepening, I figured my father would expect me to get a job after my midwinter graduation. After all, at my age he was already the principal support of his family. There was no need to discuss the matter, for it had been clear for years that the family's financial ice was quite thin.

"Dad," I said, "I need a suit to graduate in."

"What's the matter, you don't got a suit? You got a suit." European mind-set.

"But I need a new suit," I said. "I'm graduating."

"You can't graduate in your old suit?"

"Dad!"

The rental blue cap and gown. "No one will see, Sonny, underneath the blue *shmata*, it's not a new suit."

Near tears. "Dad, you don't understand!"

"Am I Rockefeller? *Nudnik!*" Pest.

The argument flared up again and again for days. I was aware, of course, that he had become the family life preserver for relatives harder hit by the Depression on the East Coast.

Al Sidney, or whatever was his professional name that day, makes a walking stick float and do midair acrobatics.

He'd helped not only his younger sister Aunt Gussie and her family resettle, but my mother's many sisters and their husbands and children as well. Our house became a principal stop in a kind of economic underground railroad. I wasn't grasping how nearly broke my father was.

One night, with the graduation date roaring down on me, Dad came home with two suits my size he'd picked out at the wholesalers. He didn't say anything about thinking things over. He just said, "*Nu*, which one do you want?"

One was a double-breasted suit with faint chalk stripes. It was love at first sight. The other was a sporty black gabardine with leather buttons. It was a suit to die for.

I tried the jackets on, one after the other, unable to make up my mind.

"I think . . . maybe the gabardine . . . no, the chalk stripes. Let me try it on again."

Suddenly, as offhandedly as if they were mere neckties, he said, "You can have both. I'll cuff the pants."

I was astounded. He'd been insensitive, and his conscience had bothered him. Had my mother pulled him aside? But I'd been self-absorbed and greedy as a pig. What did I need two suits for? Later that year, when I was out traveling, Pearl wrote me that she'd overheard Ma and Dad in whispered conversation. Their bank account had eroded to less than a hundred dollars.

I have left unsaid that during my last year in high school the abracadabra kid wrote a book. A thin book. A magic book. I'd discovered a certain knack for inventing tricks. During the summer I sat down to the family Remington and rattled out the text on a ragged blue ribbon. Mr. Jones went over my grammar, and I gave him a mention in the introduction. Dad's younger brother Sam, the sort of joking uncle all kids adore, took the photographs of my hands in action, and I thanked him, too.

Between Cocktails, my idea of a sophisticated title, was made up of tricks with paper matches that could be done informally—between cocktails. A packet of matches is made to vanish, appear, or pass through a trouser pocket. A pencil line drawn on a match magically jumps to another match and back again. That sort of thing.

The book was published when I was nineteen, and changed everything.

EXPERT
AT THE
CARD TABLE

---

*Your book would make a movie or
a soap opera. Do you think you
could use our class? Let's do lunch.*

My mother, who got both the vote and me in 1920, has almost escaped mention in these pages. She was far from invisible in real life. I remember her in the twenties in a Jazz Age blue cloche hat. I remember her in the thirties sitting poker-faced with a flush in her hands.

She was a crackerjack penny-ante cardplayer. She wouldn't have known a bottom deal from a false cut, but she had card sense. Instinct. And a strong memory. She knew the cards that had been played and seemed able to figure the odds while comparing recipes for sponge cake. Had she been born a generation later, she might have been a mathematician.

I'm convinced that during the late Depression years she helped run the house on her poker winnings. She'd go to two or three card parties a week, often dragging along Honey, still a child, who'd grow painfully bored and angry with no one to play with. Using paid baby-sitters was then a practice almost unknown.

If Ma returned home grouchy, Pearl and I knew she had

lost at the card table; there were other talented cardplayers among her friends. When she won, she sailed home, banners flying.

All of us kids hated her passion for cards, for it triggered the only shouting matches we heard our parents get into. Dad, keeping his store open seven days a week, resented her trifling away her afternoons at the card table.

"Fleischman!" she'd shout. "What do you expect me to do all day? Sit home?"

He didn't have an answer. Even worse would be if she went out and found a job. Depression or not, married women in those days didn't work outside the home. It would make embarrassingly public a husband's inability to support his family. The European in Dad would have died of shame.

On one occasion he walked out, and I didn't even know it. He worked such long hours, often keeping the store open until nine at night, that I didn't realize he was gone. Suitably chastised after a couple of days, Ma sent Pearl downtown on the streetcar to tell him to come home. He did.

Despite her protest about sitting in the house all day, she came from a generation of women who were most at home at home. She gloried in the bazaar of rich Jewish dishes that came out of her kitchen. She had a heavy hand with butter and eggs, raisins and cinnamon. And then, like a closing act in vaudeville, she'd bring forth a sponge cake or a marble cake, a hundredweight of cookies or a square yard of cinnamon apple pie. The wonder is that we kids didn't weigh a ton each, but we must have run off the calories, for I grew up skinny and Pearl even skinnier. It was a greater wonder how Ma stocked her kitchen on a Depression budget.

Ma had learned to bake from her mother, with never a

My younger sister, Honey,
age six, at a time when I gave
her a grass hula skirt for her
birthday. Given the trickeries
of memory, I recall that she
was embarrassed, hated the
garment on sight, and refused
to put it on. She recalls that
she loved it and that she
and her friends played with
it for years.
The other memories in these
pages are absolutely true.
I think.

glance at a recipe. None of the family recipes was committed to paper. They were like tribal tales handed down from generation to generation. Ingredients were measured by pinches and handfuls. Pearl and Honey once measured Ma's hand and attempted to convert the portions to cups and teaspoons and tablespoons. But the next time Ma baked, she didn't follow her earlier portions. My sisters despaired and gave it up.

Summers were a great time. Ma would pack boxes and sacks of food, and at eight in the morning Dad would drive us to Mission Beach before opening his store. We'd play all day in the sun, and he'd return for us after dark.

Like our Bauman cousins, we'd come home with neon red sunburns on the first beach day of summer. We'd blister and then peel off great patches of skin. In early summer the kids of San Diego looked as if they were molting. We never learned. The following year we'd burn all over again.

We were growing up as hothouse creatures of the California semitropics. Here snow never fell. One winter Sunday when Dad drove us to the mountains to play in the snow, Honey, age three, became so frightened that she burst into tears and wouldn't get out of the car. I was in my early twenties when I first saw snow fall. I was transfixed. I'd never seen anything so beautiful. Snow rarely appears in my stories, but when it does, it gets a good press.

Now that I had finished high school, my mother must have wondered what in the world was going to happen to me. I was the first Fleischman who couldn't baste a hem. If she had apprehensions about my future, she kept them to herself and put her trust in luck—and in me. I think she had a maternal hunch that I'd land on my feet. Plus, she was kind of smitten

65

BERT LEVEY CIRCUIT

OF

VAUDEVILLE THEATRES

Inc.

Warner Bros. Downtown Theatre Bldg.

LOS ANGELES

CALIFORNIA

Feb 26 193_8_

[This form is issued in lieu of a Bert Levey

Circuit Contract.]

Theatre _Hippodrome_

City _Los Angeles_ State _Cal_

Rehearsal Time _9:30 A_ M

Date _Feb 27 28 March 1 38_

Name of Act _Al Sidney_

No. of People _1_ Scenery _✓_

Salary _15.00_, Less _10%_

BERT LEVEY CIRCUIT
OF
VAUDEVILLE THEATRES
Inc.

Per _Adam_

Artist _Al Sidney_

with show business. She'd once had a crush on Rudolph Valentino, the silent film star.

So when I announced that I was taking my magic act to Los Angeles to try to break into vaudeville, her only concern was that I have a roof over my head. "I'll call Uncle Sam and Aunt Pearl and tell them you're coming," she said.

Uncle Sam, with eyes as pale as grapes, was the only Fleischman who spoke English without an accent. He'd arrived from Olik in Bubba's arms and grown up like a native-born. He owned an unpainted furniture store in Alhambra, a suburb east of Los Angeles. If Aunt Pearl, also Russian born, got tired of my nesting on the living room couch in their one-bedroom duplex, she never flashed any impatience.

From Alhambra I hopped the big red streetcars to downtown Los Angeles, where the booking agents kept their offices. Like other acts, I'd make the rounds each day, signing my name in reception room logs so the agents would know I was in town. "Al Sidney, magician," I'd write, adding my uncle's phone number. I didn't much like Al Sidney as a professional name, and it didn't last very long. I was to try on names like hats for the next few years.

One day the phone rang. There was a job for a magician at the Hippodrome Theater on Main Street in Los Angeles. I could play a split week of three days, five shows a day. I would be paid fifteen dollars, less the 10 percent agent's fee.

I was in.

Fresh out of high school, I broke into vaudeville.
Within a few years the footlights would be turned
off and vaudeville, with its live acrobats, slapstick
comedians, jugglers, singers, and magicians,
would disappear forever.

67

16

FOOTLIGHTS

*Chancy and the Grand Rascal
was cool. But why didn't you put
some murders and violence in it?*

I faced a problem.

The Hippodrome turned out to be a run-down vaudeville house where the booking agents caught the new acts in town.

Professional magicians, like waiters, worked in formal evening clothes. I'd look like an amateur to the bookers in my graduation suit. But I'd have to wear it. The cheapest new tuxedo I could find cost twenty-five dollars. It was out of the question. The bookers weren't going to book me.

But in my act I did the whimsical six-card trick, spinning each throwaway card over the footlights and into the audience. It was then a fresh trick and evidently unseen in vaudeville. The agents overlooked my wardrobe and booked me into neighborhood theaters that ran vaudeville on weekends to lure inside a few extra Depression customers.

I continued to sleep on the couch in Alhambra. When I got booked as a floor show act into a smart supper club, Omar's Dome, at Fourth and Hill streets, I figured the time had come to invest in evening clothes. Omar's Dome would be paying me a bountiful thirty-five dollars a week!

For ten dollars I bought a secondhand but elegant suit of tails and moved to the YMCA a few blocks from the nightclub. To freshen my act, I rigged up a pair of white silk gloves to vanish when I tossed them away.

When I walked out under the spotlight, ablaze in my white tie and tails, I felt so much like Fred Astaire the wonder was that I didn't start tap-dancing. I pulled off my white gloves, cavalierly tossed them into thin air—voilà!—and then began to make my black walking stick float before me. But the gloves caught my eye. They were dangling like dead fish from my right sleeve. They hadn't vanished at all. They'd got hung up on my starched white cuff.

I survived that mishap but not the late hours. The acts were to do three floor shows a night, the last one at eleven o'clock. Normally asleep by ten or so, I was having trouble staying awake for the final show.

One night, after the second performance, I walked back to the YMCA to rest for a few minutes. When I woke up, it was eleven-twenty. By the time I could race back to Omar's Dome, the floor show was finished. And so was I. I moved back to my uncle's living room couch.

I kept myself in small change by doing "casuals"—single performances at service club banquets or parties. A booker from a small agency phoned: "Wanna do a kid's birthday party out in Beverly Hills?"

"Sure," I said.

"It only pays two-fifty."

"Oh."

"Better take it. It's Mark Sandrich's kid."

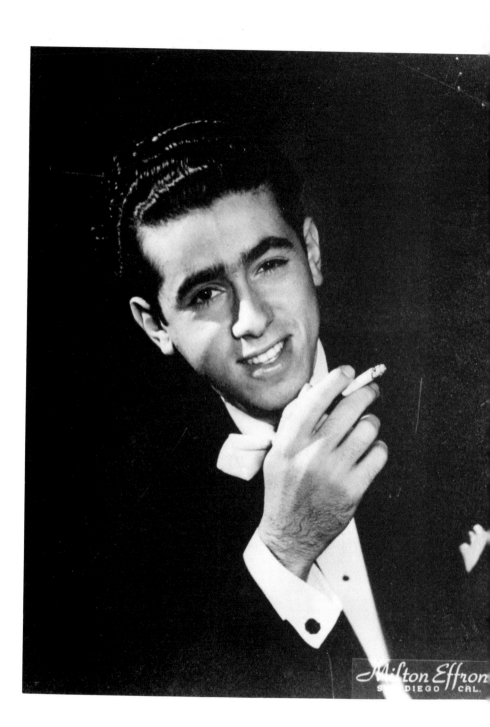

70

"Who's Mark Sandrich?"

"The movie director. Those Astaire, Ginger Rogers pictures. He might put you in one of his movies. It may be your break."

So I went out to Beverly Hills and did my stuff for young Jay Sandrich's party. Instead of mailing the fee to the agency, Mrs. Sandrich made a five-dollar check out to me. Hadn't she made an error? "It's only two-fifty."

"The agent said five dollars," she insisted.

The thief! Not only was the booker stealing half the performance fee, but he expected to collect an additional 10 percent agent's commission on my remaining pittance. I was outraged. I stopped off at his office, told him his felony was a hanging offense, and left the fifty-cent commission he was entitled to. He never booked me again. Mark Sandrich didn't put me in pictures, either.

Aunt Pearl got her living room couch back hours after a telegram turned up from Buddy. Graduating a year before me, he'd got a job as a stage assistant in the Francisco Spook & Magic Show. Buddy was lovesick for a girlfriend he'd left behind in California. Would I replace him in the show?

I took a Greyhound bus and caught up with the show in Denver.

In my ten-dollar suit of tails. I didn't smoke, but like most magicians of that day, I performed the act of catching lit cigarettes out of thin air.

(Photo credit: Milton Effron)

17
THE SPOOK SHOW

*Maybe if you write a book all about
me, just me, and I become famous
I'll even go to Hollywood or Broadway.*

Isaac Bashevis Singer has said that an author needs an address. For the next two years I was in a different town almost every night, largely in the Midwest. There I stumbled across the story address for several novels and particularly the McBroom tall tales.

The spook show was in perpetual motion, playing one-night stands in small-town movie theaters. Francisco, the ghost raiser, was a six-foot gentlemanly graying magician. As one of two stage assistants, I wore a red jacket with brass buttons.

The spook show swung open its curtains at midnight, bringing forth phosphorescent bats and glowing goblins for the last ten minutes of what was essentially a program of off-the-rack magic tricks.

Like theater raffles, bank night drawings, and free dishes, spook shows were creatures of the Depression. By staging performances after the last movie ended, when the house normally went dark, the seats could be sold again. For the theater owner it was found money.

A handbill for the midnight spook frolic at the time I joined the show. For the price of admission, now parking meter change, one got a live stage show and a scary movie, generally something starring Boris Karloff or Bela Lugosi.

For small-town teenagers the arrival of a spook show was Halloween all over again. They flocked to the box office at midnight. In the darkened theater, seated beside girlfriends or boyfriends, they'd be scared into screaming embraces—or eagerly pretended to be.

We rehearsed in Denver for only a day, enabling me to learn my stage routine, and rushed on to the next performance date in Pueblo. I thought the show was so bad I was almost too embarrassed to venture onstage. It was just a bunch of mechanical tricks. Anyone could do them.

We packed the show and performed the next night in La Junta. Wild jubilation. Trinidad, shouts for more. By the time we crossed into Kansas, it dawned on me that this might be the best magic show on the road. The box tricks were knocking the audiences dead. The theaters rocked. Hands applauded. No one missed the subtle and exotic sleight of hand that I contemplated instead of my navel. From that moment on, I began having the time of my life.

Francisco was Arthur Bull, a native of San Francisco (thus his stage name), who'd started professional life as a wooden leg maker. Going bust in the mail-order truss business during the Depression, he'd parlayed his magic hobby into a scare-and-mystery show and, late in life, created a new career. He proved to be the most successful of the spook show magicians.

Devoted as I became to Arthur, I adored his wife, Mabel. Almost as tall as he, openhearted and motherly, she somehow managed to dress stylishly out of a suitcase. We traveled like a family in a 1938 Plymouth, pulling the entire show in a two-wheel trailer.

The common car radio was then unborn. We spent the long travel hours talking, reading, and watching the prairie pass in slow motion. Arthur loved to recall wooden leg stories from his youth.

"Sid, did I tell you about my friend Charlie Hastings? He had a leg off below the left knee, so he didn't limp so anyone would notice. Up against hard times, Charlie stepped into a bar and made it known that he was a wonderful freak of nature. He could feel no pain. He bet he could drive an ice pick through his leg without springing a tear. When enough cash built up on the bar, he borrowed the bartender's ice pick and hammered it through his left calf. Strong men fainted away. Charlie walked out with a bankroll. But the next time he tried it, the ice pick split open that expensive leg of his. It finished his career as a con artist."

Taking turns at the wheel, we crisscrossed Kansas and Nebraska. Arriving in a show town, we'd stop at the theater to pick up our mail, set up the show, and rehearse the stooges. Stooges?

In the blackout sequence, just before the final curtain (despite fire regulations, even the exit lights were turned out), apparitions would appears. Wraiths and skulls would glow all over the theater. Those spirits weren't wisps of genuine ectoplasm. They were a dozen or so local boys, sworn to secrecy, whom we'd rehearsed to march down the aisles while holding aloft phosphorous images painted on corrugated cardboard.

The stagecraft looked good. In complete darkness we lose our depth perception. The dead appeared to be floating everywhere.

But this ghostly Grand Guignol could be a risky affair. The secret got out, and sometimes on the show's return engagements a couple of delinquent boys would tie a rope across the

Arthur Bull, master of the ghostly revels, stands before the car that transported us from one-night stand to one-night stand. The entire stage show packed down into the two-wheeled trailer.

aisle, ankle high, and gleefully wait in the dark. Along came our unsuspecting ghosts. And suddenly feet tripped on the rope. There'd be a football pileup. Ectoplasm would fly loose and go sailing all over the theater. No one ever got hurt. Despite discovering that the spooks were mere cardboard when the lights came up, the kids didn't ask for their money back.

It was somewhere in Nebraska, I think, that we stepped into a hotel elevator and I heard someone say, "Jim don't know sic 'em from fetch 'em."

What language was this? Didn't they speak English in Nebraska? And Missouri? Or Iowa? Here someone might be ugly as homemade soap. Someone else was plain as poverty. Or uppity as a hog on ice.

This isn't the way we talked at home. I had a date with a box-office cashier, who said she loved my California accent. What accent? She said Paderewski played the *pie-ana*. *Yellow* ended in a consonant.

With my antenna up, I began to eavesdrop on the country argot. When these midwesterners needed a simile or metaphor, they turned to the barnyard and seemed to roll their own. Someone was as hot as a hen laying a goose egg. Or wet as water snakes. Their imagery was funnier than ours and more creative. Useless as eating soup with a fork. So dry you could spit cotton. Nervous as a long-tailed cat in a room full of rocking chairs.

My sense of the color of language was awakened. Had I known how this would affect my writing style, I might have taken notes. But I was like someone riding backward on a train who couldn't see where he was going but had a clear view of where he had been.

I *had* begun to think about writing. By the time I joined the show, I'd read all of O. Henry and de Maupassant. With their surprise endings, the stories struck me as literary magic tricks. Maybe I'd try my hand at one one of these days.

18

THE LITTLE
SHOP OF
HOCUS POCUS

---

*Please answer my questions to
the fullest of your ability.*

We had a week's layover in Chicago, and Arthur let me drive
the car over to minuscule Colon, Michigan. There an Australian conjurer named Percy Abbott had founded a trick-fabricat-
ing and book-publishing company that became the magic
capital of the world. A couple of months earlier I had sent
him the manuscript of *Between Cocktails*. The long silence was
beginning to feel ominous.

Arthur needed a special prop for the show, so I happily
volunteered to make the drive to Colon. Until Abbott came
along, magic secrets were largely self-published in the form
of mimeographed manuscripts. In any year we were lucky to
see a half dozen professionally printed and bound new books.
Once Abbott installed a couple of printing presses, a luxuriant
library of printed secrets came pouring out of Colon, Michigan.

"Didn't my letter catch up with you, Sid?" said Percy Abbott,
flashing a vaudevillian's smile. He stood in summer shirtsleeves, friendly but reserved. His reputation was that of a
wily businessman.

"No, sir." I didn't know what to make of the smile. To soften the blow?

"Well, your book's not up there with Jean Hugard and Ted Annemann."

Big magic names. "No, sir."

"What do you want for it?"

Was he considering publishing the book? "I don't know. What do you suggest, Mr. Abbott?"

"How about fifty dollars?"

"That sounds fine to me."

"In trade."

"Okay."

"All rights?"

"Yours."

He could have paid off in sand dollars. What did it matter? He *was* going to publish me! I quickly picked out some magic equipment, including the prop for Arthur, and fled before the sainted man came to his senses.

My life with the show went on. As we drove into St. Louis on a rainy morning, a car cut us off, we swerved, and the show trailer was pitched onto its side. The magic props were a bit shaken. At the theater Arthur went around with a hammer and nails to tighten box joints and whatnot.

During the show that night I was locked inside a box, inside a curtained cabinet. I was to escape. There was a trap in the rear of the box through which I made my exit. But not in St. Louis.

I had a pencil flashlight with me and a small tool that opened the trap. I held the flashlight between my teeth, found the secret release, inserted the tool, and pulled at the trap. It wouldn't open. I tugged. I jimmied. I yanked. I sweated.

"Arthur! I'm locked in! The trap won't open!"

He shut the cabinet curtain, took a moment to review the situation, and kicked the trap open. I emerged like a wet fish with the flashlight between my teeth.

He looked at me and shrugged, before going on with the show. "Some damned fool nailed the trap shut," he said.

I was paid four dollars per performance, with the show picking up the hotel and restaurant bills. The second year, the pay was lifted to six dollars, luxuriant by Depression standards.

By that time printed copies of *Between Cocktails* had reached me. I looked at my name on the cover. This was heady stuff for a nineteen-year-old. *By Sid Fleischman.* Imagine. It was like having one's name in lights. At that moment I knew I wanted to change direction.

I'd made a couple of blind leaps into short fiction but got thoroughly lost. Writing stories was harder than it looked. And hadn't I better go to college and get decently educated? But what would I use for money?

In the backseat of the Plymouth I'd devised a new way of making a white handkerchief float from the magician's hand. Maybe I could earn some college money by marketing the trick. I fancifully advertised it in the magic magazines as the "Million Dollar Gimmick." Price, one dollar.

I named my company the Little Shop of Hocus Pocus. Little? It was a card table in my bedroom at home in San Diego. On the road I'd make up the secret gimmicks and send them home. As they flocked in, my mother filled the orders. And in they did flock. This trick and others that followed kept me in college for the next two years.

As for *Between Cocktails*, it remained in print for the next fifty years.

THICKENING
THE PLOT

I loved your book
Ramona.

I enrolled at San Diego State College one windy January day. I was sorry to leave the spook show, and Arthur and Mabel, who kept touring for another ten years.

State, now a huge and cosmopolitan university, was then so small that the student body was outnumbered by jackrabbits. All red tile roofs and white stucco, the college stood in Spanish Colonial splendor on one of the mesquite- and cactus-spiked hills behind San Diego.

Fiction writing wasn't taught. I sat through freshman English and quickly sensed that story construction, the nuts and bolts of fiction, was regarded as one of the manual arts. No one in the fine arts seemed to know how it was done.

Well, I was an autodidact, wasn't I? I'd taught myself sleight of hand, hadn't I? Again I hit the library stacks, and behold, there waiting for me sat books on story-writing techniques. After reading through the downtown shelves of the main library, I scouted out the branches. I wasn't finding exactly what I wanted.

I read about opening lines with hooks in them to catch the browser's attention. I got advice on how to create atmosphere and how to write dialogue, and I was warned about a million things to avoid. In fact there seemed to be so many pitfalls, invisible to the naked eye, that I was almost afraid to attempt a story—assuming that I could find an idea for one.

One author said that when he needed a story idea, he'd find one in the classified ads. So I began to skim classified ads. But I didn't have the skill to pry a story out of someone with a used bathtub for sale or someone else named Boo Hoo asking Jersey Jim to telephone. I didn't know how to make a plot.

And the books weren't telling me. If there was a big secret to writing fiction, not shared with us bedeviled beginners, that appeared to be it. Or perhaps the authors of these writing texts themselves didn't know how it was done.

Daily life doesn't often help. It rarely delivers us three acts ready to write. The author needs to rearrange the furniture, putting random story elements in some sort of dramatic alignment. The trouble is that every time you write page one, you face a wild new set of variables.

The puzzlements of plotting probably sink more writers than any other element in the creative enigma. I know professional writers who confess, in embarrassed whispers, that they don't know how to plot. Evidently they have dramatic sense and trust to luck that when they finish, someone will find some architecture lurking around in their pages. It's as spooky as trying to ride a bicycle without a sense of balance.

But Shakespeare knew how to plot. And so did Dickens and Wilde and Dostoevsky and Twain. I hung in there, waiting for some incandescent moment to come along when I would suddenly understand.

While fiction writing wasn't taught at State, fiction reading was all over the catalog. I lucked into a literature class taught by a courteous young professor with a freshly minted doctorate, John Adams.

I doubt that Dr. Adams had ever attempted to write a line of fiction. He would have agreed with the wit Fred Allen who didn't know why anyone would spend a year or two writing a novel when you can easily buy one for a few dollars.

But Dr. Adams gave us freshmen literary oxygen. With an owlish smile, he taught us nuance and subtlety and the pleasures of the right word. He taught me to read all over again.

And as I was reading widely, I began fooling around with style. I tried writing Henry James sentences, but it was too much like pulling taffy, and I settled on the quicker pulse of Hemingway prose, trim and unpretentious.

In those days I was no literary diamond in the rough—I wasn't even a zircon—but Dr. Adams seemed to take my aspirations seriously. I remember one humiliating day when, in another English class, the instructor returned one of my book reports with an angry D minus. Her scribbled note proclaimed she'd have given the paper an A, but she was quite certain I had copied it. She'd been unable to find the source of my plagiarism, or she'd have let me have an F between the eyes.

I was as hot under the collar as the day I was cheated by the booking agent in Los Angeles. I found her in her office and let off ten minutes of live steam. She wasn't convinced. She said coolly she'd take the matter up with her colleague Dr. Adams.

I stewed until she called me into her office a couple of days later. Dr. Adams had read the report and said flatly I'd written it. She changed my grade, but it was too late to matter. My sense of injustice was aroused. I'm still sore.

The Little Shop of Hocus Pocus was thriving. Every mail brought two or three letters, each with a dollar bill stuffed inside, ordering my handkerchief gimmick. I followed it up with a fresh trick every couple of months. At night I was slipping into my white tie and tails to play one of the local boozy nightclubs, of which there were many. But when I was booked into the classy La Mesa Country Club, Ma and Dad turned up to make sure I hadn't fallen into the hands of gangsters. The club was paying me too much to be honest. I was getting a lavish thirty-five dollars a week.

Out into the spotlight stepped Fred Astaire doing his magic tricks. Dad had already recognized a local judge at one of the tables and decided the club must be legit. I could see him in the semidarkness, smiling. As they were leaving, Dad turned to me for the briefest of moments and said, "You were pretty good, Sid."

I was floored. That was as close to a laurel leaf as I'd known Dad to hand out. Furthermore, he rarely called me Sonny again.

But he was right about the club. I was there for weeks before a blond young man in a tux came up to me one night after the last show. I'd seen him lurking around the place. He asked for my deck of cards and did the best bottom deals I'd ever seen. He gave a little laugh, returned my cards, and vanished. He needed to show off his secret skill to me.

For the first time I learned that the club hosted illegal gambling in a back room. He was one of the dealers.

20

ENTER, THE GIRL FROM LONG BEACH

Is you married?

Meanwhile, the world was going mad. Hitler burst into France and gave a little dance step. Lindbergh got on the radio and we heard Nazi swastikas come flying out of his mouth. He blamed everything wrong in Europe on the British and the Jews.

Was this Lucky Lindy, the tall American from Minnesota who'd flown the Atlantic all alone in his little silver-nosed plane built in San Diego, *The Spirit of St. Louis*? Could that hero of our childhoods now be strutting with a goose step? I felt searingly betrayed. He'd grown horns and a tail. In a flash I loathed him.

I already carried a draft card in my pocket, but we would not be in the war for another year. With one eye always cocked on the events unfolding in Europe, our lives raced on.

I'd been reading Prescott's vivid account of Cortez's conquest of Mexico for one of my classes, and my eyes had been opened to cosmic human greed, cunning, superstition, and cruelty. This was history as bloody theater, with strutting players in rich costumes leaving more dead piled on the stage than Shakespeare had felled in *Hamlet*. In the summer of 1941 my cousin Seymour and I drove in his Chevy to Mexico City to take a direct look at history.

But you needed X-ray vision to see through the asphalt and swirling traffic to the Aztec sites buried by the centuries. Where had the terrible night, the famous *noche triste*, taken place? There? It was hard to see the sixteenth-century Spaniards fleeing the city across a broken causeway, piling up and crawling over one another in a human lava flow.

But the Aztec pyramids were being freshly unearthed, and we climbed them, as did a girl from San Diego State who was spending the summer at the University of Mexico. Accident did not bring us together.

But when I returned to college that fall, a friend introduced me to a slim girl in a pink angora sweater and saddle shoes who was just back from her adventures in Mexico City. She was a Spanish-language major with watercolor green eyes named Betty Taylor. We began going together. Before long we were auditing each other's classes to be together an extra hour or so. By that time we had discovered that angora sheds.

And she had a good figure for stage tights. A couple of my friends had put their girlfriends into their magic acts. When I suggested she join me on the stage, Betty arched an eyebrow and fixed me with a bemused green gaze. "Sid, darling, you're either crazy or you're out of your mind." And that was that.

A couple of months later Japan bombed Pearl Harbor, and we were in World War II. I had already joined the U.S. Naval Reserve, deciding against the army, as I liked the idea even in war of sleeping between clean white sheets. Two days after the bombing in Hawaii, I was called up for active duty.

I skipped boot camp, where I would have learned how to tie square knots and other seagoing skills. When the navy discovered I could type—not primitive hunt-and-peck typing, but with all ten fingers—I was rushed into the recruiting service. Volunteers in patriotic tidal waves were hitting the recruiting stations. Paperwork in daily blizzards needed processing. Boot camp would have to wait.

I was given a petty officer's rating, yeoman third class, and locked to a clattering Underwood typewriter. When eventually I shipped out, it escaped notice that I had not been trained at boot camp. I wonder if I am the only sailor who ever went to war unsure which side of the ship was port and which was starboard.

The war accelerated our lives, and we didn't need a Gypsy to read our tea leaves. There was going to be overseas duty. On January 25 Betty and I drove to Yuma, Arizona, and returned in the middle of the night married. She was twenty. I was twenty-one.

We knew our parents would be upset, but at least we avoided trench warfare at the wedding ceremony. There had not been a Jew in Betty's family in recorded history. There had not been a Gentile in mine.

Our mothers, both realists, made peace at once. Betty's Kansas-born father must have bitten through his ivory cigarette holder. My father didn't speak to me for a year.

The common footnotes to our lives, as I'd discovered with touch typing and the navy, can affect our destinies. Betty, growing up with a divorced and rancorous mother, had been taught to sew by a beloved grandmother. Whatever Betty did, she did extremely well. When my father saw the exquisitely made doll clothes she sewed for my niece, Carol, he was impressed. This girl's stitches were a wonder! She was his match with the needle. He thawed out at once, and they remained devoted friends for the rest of their lives.

And Betty's father and I became friends. He wanted me to take over from him in managing a small oil company in Long Beach, a hundred miles to the north, where Betty had grown

Eating Cracker Jack in Central Park. Betty and I had just arrived in Manhattan, where I was attached to the recruiting service. We found an apartment on East Fifty-sixth Street.

up. I told him that I hadn't an ounce of business sense, but he was willing to overlook it. It was only after I began publishing books that he gave me up as a lost cause in the world of petroleum.

War or no war, I continued trying to write fiction. I'd spring-load clever surprise endings into my stories and mail them off to the popular magazines of the day, the *Saturday Evening Post*, *Collier's*, and *Liberty*. Meanwhile, the navy transferred me to the recruiting station at 383 Madison Avenue in New York. A few floors above us were the editorial offices of a major book publisher, Harcourt, Brace and Company.

It was no wonder I would one day step into an elevator and discover Carl Sandburg standing there. He'd undoubtedly been upstairs to see his publisher.

Betty and I had subleased an apartment on East Fifty-sixth Street. I took time from evening fiction writing to work on a government-sponsored correspondence course in mathematics. While I had two years of college, I lacked the math necessary to qualify for officer candidate school. I really wasn't interested in advancing myself in the military (how much longer, after the past couple of years, could the war last?), but I was tired of typing up enlistment papers.

The notion of becoming a commissioned officer—the kind you salute, instead of the petty officer I was, who initiates the saluting—vanished when a letter arrived from *Liberty*. The editor liked the story I sent and would pay $250 to publish it.

I'd climbed the Alps! I'd sold a story at last! I was right up there with O. Henry and de Maupassant and Hemingway and F. Scott Fitzgerald. I put away my correspondence course and never worked another math problem. Someone else could wear the gold braid. I lost interest in the war. I was a fiction writer.

But the war hadn't lost interest in me. I received orders to pack my seabag and to head for Norfolk, Virginia, to help put my ship, just launched, in commission.

I would no longer be living ashore. This was sea duty. Betty and I spent hours flipping the pages of my *Bluejackets' Manual*, trying to figure out how to tie a square knot, the regulation way to fold navy clothing, and the other peculiar skills I was presumed to have mastered.

21

REPERTORY
COMPANY
OF WARRIORS

*I don't like your stories.
You use those weird words.*

I arrived in Norfolk, but my newly hatched warship was not at anchor in the bay waiting for me. It was detained at the Brooklyn Navy Yard for some last-minute design changes. The torpedo tube was being removed from the afterdeck and replaced with a gun turret.

Nevertheless, the ship's skeleton crew gathered and set up shop at the naval base. I met the captain, a short, solid, bulldog-faced officer named Sidney King. He looked ferocious. He turned out to be not only an officer and a gentleman but a good guy with a lurking sense of humor.

Day by day and week by week our repertory company of warriors turned up: gunners, radiomen, signalmen, the engineering gang who would vanish belowdecks, cooks, bakers, boilermakers, junior officers, yeomen, machinist's mates, storekeepers, radar and sonar operators, carpenters, the boatswain, a flock of able-bodied seamen, and the executive officer, Lieutenant Commander William E. Byrne. In civilian life he had managed a Chicago five-and-ten-cent store, a background

91

that at first didn't inspire great confidence as second-in-command of the ship. Once we were at sea, it quickly became apparent that he was the most competent man aboard.

It also became apparent that our baker couldn't bake. His bread was so stiff and sawdusty you needed a hacksaw to slice it. When you bit off a piece, you looked for splinters. He made no secret of his hatred of the kitchen. Built like a football player, he yearned to be a gunner's mate. As a civilian he'd once worked briefly in a bakery. The navy must have been as short of bakers as typists, for he was doomed to wear on his sleeve the half-moon insignia of cooks and bakers.

He was too embarrassed to go on liberty with that tell-all half-moon on his sleeve. Before going ashore, he'd get one of the gunners to loan him *his* jacket to wear in public.

We were months in Norfolk waiting for our ship. Betty, working as a secretary for an import-export firm, remained behind in Manhattan. Suddenly I got a telegram. She was on her way to Norfolk. She'd quit her job.

Housing was almost impossible to find, but Betty turned up a room in a private home. We were reunited for a while.

To polish the crew's survival skills, we were marched to the shooting range, where a chief petty officer lectured us. "Lower the sight to the bull's-eye. Take your time. Buffalo Bill never rushed. Now slowly, slowly squeeze the trigger. Don't jerk. Squeeze." Bang! Bull's-eye!

When I stepped up to the range, the chief placed a loaded pistol into my hand. The only gun I'd shot before was a friend's BB air rifle as a kid. I was surprised at how heavy the pistol felt.

I did what the chief said. I took my time. Slowly, slowly I squeezed. Like Buffalo Bill. Bang! I looked at the target. Where was the hole? I must have missed it entirely. I tried again. And again. Slowly. Like Buffalo Bill. Squeeze. Bang!

When I'd emptied the clip, the target was released and came traveling on a wire toward me. The chief caught sight of it and gave me a surprised look. The small black bull's-eye was shot full of holes. Only two of the ten bullets had strayed off center. For the rest of the war I was regarded, in some awe, as the sharpshooting Buffalo Bill of our ship. I never admitted my mere BB gun past, and I was wise enough not to attempt a sharpshooting encore. I quit while I was ahead.

At last we received orders to man our ship. Officers and crew, as well as Betty and a few other wives, piled into gritty old train cars, and off we rattled, north to the Brooklyn Navy Yard.

22
SHAKEDOWN CRUISE

*I especially like
those crazy words.*

The first time I saw the sleek USS *Albert T. Harris,* I thought the ship looked as touchy and snappish as a crocodile. In lightning-strike war paint, it carried five-inch cannon fore and aft; that's to say they fired shells five inches in *diameter.* Built as a submarine hunter, the ship was loaded with depth charges in fifty-gallon drums racked and waiting on the fantail, the rear end. A flight of small bombs, called hedgehogs, lay snugged quietly forward. Antiaircraft guns—the ones that go ack! ack! ack!—swung in small, circular steel balconies port and starboard. I finally committed it to memory: Port was the left side, starboard the right.

The *Albert T. Harris,* DE 447, was named for a young naval lieutenant from Georgia killed earlier in the Pacific war in the Solomon Islands. The *DE* before her number identified the ship as a destroyer escort. Like bodyguards, we would be escorting convoys of lightly armed supply ships across war zone waters.

The plan must have looked good on paper. While the ship was bristling with sophisticated weaponry, the officers and

I sent home this picture of my ship, DE 447.
(A) indicated the flying bridge, where I stood
watch as the captain's talker. (B) was the ship's
office, where, among other duties, I wrote and
mimeographed the ship's newspaper. (C) was
where I slept, right next to the ship's ammunition.

crew were out of Gilbert and Sullivan. Hardly any of us had
been to sea before, and that included the captain. On our
shakedown cruise to Bermuda we were struck by furious seas
off Cape Hatteras. Except for three old salts with gyroscope
stomachs, everyone aboard was white-faced seasick. We hung
over the rails like sailors in a comedy skit, throwing up into
the wind and everywhere else.

I got little of my yeoman's paperwork done in the ship's

office. Sick or not, we had to stand our watches. I felt only moderately queasy as long as I lay flat on my back, all the while trying to get down dry soda crackers. I remember klaxon horns sounding an ear-piercing general quarters; were there dumb enemy ships out in this storm?

I rolled off my bunk and made a wobbly, seasick climb to my battle station on the flying bridge. That's where the captain would be, and there he was, looking pale as a corpse. He was peering off into the storm. I thought I got a flash of a dark, foamy submarine surfaced off the port side.

I was so eager to lie down again I would have been glad to surrender. I rushed to the starboard side and again heaved everything I'd eaten since the Brooklyn Navy Yard. I wiped my chin on the sleeve of my peacoat and clamped on earphones and mouthpiece. During general quarters my job was to function as the captain's talker. I was wired to all parts of the ship and conveyed his orders and their reports.

If the submarine was the enemy, I didn't see how we were going to be able to knock it out. Our ship was lurching and rolling and pitching like a rubber-legged drunk. Our gunners would be lucky to land a hit on the Atlantic Ocean.

The ship out there was an enemy, all right. It was an Italian submarine with a diving problem, and she wanted to surrender to *us*.

The all-clear finally sounded, and those of us not on regular watch could get back to our bunks. Mine was right next to the ship's powder magazine.

It never cost me a moment's restlessness that all separating me from tons of explosives was a bulkhead, a metal wall. At the same time my life preserver had been stolen before we set to sea, and I went through the rest of the war without one. It never occurred to me that I might not survive. I was young enough and simpleminded enough to feel immortal. I don't think war would be possible without this sort of cosmic denial. We all felt immortal.

In those towering seas it would have been impossible to board the sub. She may have tagged along behind us to Bermuda to surrender there, though I don't recall seeing her again. I think our navy must have dispatched a saltier ship to bring in the Italians. I was too distracted by personal affliction to care.

By the time we tied up in Hamilton, Bermuda, our stomachs had steadied, and we crawled out of our bunks willing to live. I spent Christmas Day 1944 sight-seeing, and stopped to gaze at the island home of the American playwright I idolized, Eugene O'Neill.

I was never seasick again.

DESTINATION UNKNOWN

When did you start writing?
When are you going to stop?

I think Captain King regarded it as a triumph that we returned from our shakedown cruise without having run the ship aground. The navy tightened a few bolts, gave the machinery a fresh squirt of oil, and sent us up to New London, Connecticut, for a final trial. It was here that Captain King revealed himself to be an endearing and irascible civilian.

He had been a navy pilot with more than four thousand hours in the air. According to shipboard rumor, he'd begun to drink heavily and been grounded for years. When the war broke out, he had racked up so much time on shore duty that he *had* to be sent to sea. By that time he had risen to the rank of lieutenant commander. Assigned to the *Harris*, he had little personal experience with ships. But his rank was so high that he *had* to be made captain. That, we believed, was how Sidney King came to be skipper of the DE 447.

I got a clear fix on him as we were steaming into New London during a heavy fog. I was just coming on watch when he said, "Fleischman, run downstairs and get my glasses."

Downstairs? On a navy ship? Even I, civilian to the core, had learned that ships don't have stairs. They have ladders.

Hardly an hour later, as we felt our way like a blind man into the bay, he became increasingly anxious. Suddenly I saw him position his palms about ten inches apart, give them a shake, and call out, "Park it here! Park it here!"

Park it? Park a ship? I knew then I was going to feel at home on the DE 447.

It was clear that the few regular navy men aboard regarded us landlubbers as hardly more than temporary help dressed up in costume party sailor suits. The bosun (short for boatswain, the straw boss of the deckhands) was the loudest, most scornful, and least original of our tormentors. "I can wash more salt water out of my socks than you jokers have sailed on," he'd say, exercising his passion for nautical clichés.

Little did we expect what this sea-wise navy man had up his sleeve. Or foot, really.

Betty and other wives and family members showed up for the ceremony that placed the ship in commission. An admiral spoke, a band played, the ship's flags were unfurled, a buffet was laid out, and it was open house aboard the *Albert T. Harris*. The next day we would be sailing with sealed orders to the war.

But not the bosun. He'd waited for the last moment to reveal a bloody red case of eczema covering his feet and ankles. He wouldn't be going to the war. He'd beat the system. He was shipped off to the naval hospital, and a quick replacement was found.

It was my first experience with in-your-face hypocrisy, with me-first cunning aboard ship, and a final blow to my innocence. Lord Acton had almost got it right. Life corrupts. Real life really corrupts.

Betty and I embraced and whispered our last good-byes. She'd be staying on in an apartment we'd found on West Tenth in Greenwich Village. If I were lucky, maybe my ship would be stationed on the Atlantic, and I might get back to Manhattan from time to time.

Once at sea the captain opened his orders. A bosun's whistle sounded over the intercom. "Now hear this! Now hear this!" And then the captain himself addressed us. "We are ordered to the Panama Canal. Later orders will follow."

That meant we would be nosing our way into the Pacific Ocean and the war with Japan. I wouldn't be getting back to Manhattan and Betty after all.

24

LIFE AMONG
THE FLOATING
MINES

*My uncle was in the war.
Did you know him?*

The Panama Canal disgorged us out into the Pacific Ocean, where I felt right at home. We paused to take on fuel in the bleak Galápagos Islands. I was dimly aware that somewhere in these South American waters Alexander Selkirk had been marooned, inspiring the tale of Robinson Crusoe. I wondered if someday I might use these remote, moody islands as story background, and made a few mental notes. Rocky. Scraggly yellow weeds. Sharks in the bay.

At sea again, the captain opened a new set of sealed orders. He set our course for Bora Bora in the Society Islands, wherever they were.

Oh, yes, the snarling Captain Bligh and the famous mutiny on the *Bounty*—that happened in the Society Islands. At Tahiti. We'd all seen the movie with Clark Gable and Charles Laughton. I was beginning to see the world, as a writer should.

I loved being at sea. I loved the raw smell of it and the 360-degree sunsets and the costume glitter of stars at night. I'd got my sea legs and clung like a tree frog whenever the ship rolled and pitched.

I loved being at sea except for assorted torments. There was no fresh milk, and I was a milk drinker. What suffering! There were cans of condensed milk aboard, and I tried the stuff on my cereal—once. After that I poured water on my cornflakes.

I didn't drink coffee—especially navy coffee, widely referred to aboard ship as battery acid, java, or paint thinner. It tasted to me like asphalt. I made do with tea and lemon. Long before we reached the Society Islands, the ship ran out of lemons. War was hell.

When we steamed under the towering green headland into the bay at Bora Bora, I could see at once that I was gazing at the most beautiful island in the world. And it was especially hospitable to me.

Going ashore, I saw an immense lime tree growing wild and thorny along the shore. I could see a few last limes beyond reach in the lofty top branches. A boy came along and seemed to understand my dilemma. He took my sailor cap, climbed to the top, and filled the cap with glossy green limes. I gave him an American fifty-cent piece, and for weeks to come I was able to enjoy a civilized cup of tea and lime when I stood watch on the flying bridge at night.

It was only when we steamed farther into the western Pacific that I became aware of a new torment we faced at sea: floating mines.

These appeared to be about the size of volleyballs armed all around with deadly nipples. If your ship touched one of the nipples enough to compress it, the mine exploded.

As we began to patrol in the waters north of New Guinea and the Dutch East Indies (now Indonesia), the mines became an almost daily affliction. I remember once standing at the rail, casually looking down at the water, when I saw a mine come drifting by—hardly a yard from the ship. I let out a yell, but all we could do was watch the thing and hold our breaths. Miraculously it slipped into our foaming wake without touching us. Warships had standing orders to blow them up. But that was not so easily done, at least for us.

I can remember spending half a morning on one occasion trying to blow up a single stubborn mine. We fired off the ack-ack guns with tracers—round after round. The mine arrogantly kept bobbing along. In frustration, and for useful target practice, we lobbed a couple of five-inch shells at it. The mine seemed indestructible. When finally the gunners scored a hit and the device exploded, we set up a victorious yell that must have carried across the international date line.

During the day our lookouts were especially on the lookout for floating mines, of course, but what about the nights? At night we crossed our fingers and tried not to think about them.

The DE 447 did her level best to help win the war, by staying afloat, if not by any notable derring-do. We took part in two invasions in the southern Philippines, giving us a chance to fire off our five-inch guns in earnest. I'm sure we hit a couple of coconut trees, at least. I don't think anyone got hurt.

A third operation was a bit more interesting. We were ordered south from the Philippines, destination unknown, but clearly something major was happening. There were heavy-hitting cruisers in our convoy, troopships, destroyers, and a hornet's swarm of small, fast PT boats. We sailed under strict radio silence. Messages were passed between ships entirely by hand: flashing lights or skivvy waving. *Skivvy* is a navy term for underwear. Because they can pass messages with hand-

With shipmates in the South Pacific. I'm the one standing.

held flags, signalmen are called skivvy wavers.

"Now hear this!" called out the bosun over the intercom. We stopped whatever we were doing to give an ear.

"This is the captain speaking." said the skipper, and then his voice lowered as if he didn't want to chance being overheard in Tokyo. "Our destination is Borneo."

So we would be invading Borneo.

Another bit of seagoing slang is *scuttlebutt*, meaning rumor or gossip. And despite radio silence, scuttlebutt raced through the ship that the Japanese fleet was rushing at flank speed to intercept us. How could we know? Wouldn't the Japanese fleet be under radio silence as well? It was transparently nuts. A fearful fantasy.

But when I turned in that night, I saw many of my shipmates still awake in their bunks. They had dug into their seabags for the pocket Bibles issued to them on enlistment and were solemnly reading. They believed the scuttlebutt.

It was spooky. Had I better find a life preserver after all? Could the scuttlebutt be true? Hadn't someone better tell the captain? Aw, keep your head on straight, Sid. I gave a firm shrug, crawled into my sack next to the powder magazine, and I went to sleep.

The phantom Japanese fleet never turned up. And I never saw the pocket Bibles in public view again.

We threw our popgun firepower into the general bombardment of Brunei, to soften up resistance for the invasion that followed a few hours later. The shoreline lit up like a hit on a fireworks factory. A couple of Japanese planes appeared briefly and fled for the interior. Our PT boats dashed about the bay, as light on their feet as ballet dancers.

The troops, Australian and Dutch as well as American, waded ashore. A destroyer escort came limping in and would be out of service for repairs; she had struck a floating mine outside the bay. The crew at the rails was ecstatic. The mine was a ticket home. By afternoon the invasion was a done deal, we had anchored, and I was reading a book in the shade.

Some three weeks later we returned on patrol. Liberty parties were allowed to go ashore to a small, blasted island in the bay. I was struck by a pyramid that had grown up mushroom-quick in the center of the island. It was a towering monument of American and Australian beer cans.

GONE
FISHING

That story's a bummer.
Next time you should make a story like
The Blob That Ate New York.

The war seemed to have vanished. For nine days we had been lazily steaming back and forth, patrolling the San Bernardino Strait in the Philippines. There was fishing gear aboard, and a couple of guys had tried trolling, but our speed scattered away the fish.

The captain agreed to anchor for a couple of hours. A little rest and recreation wouldn't be out of order, and it would be nice to have fresh fish for dinner. Of course the anchored ship would be a sitting duck, but things were completely dead out here at the mouth of the San Bernardino Strait.

I don't recall if anyone had a fish dinner or not. When we finally steamed back to our base in Samar, the vast blue bay was wall to wall in warships. There were immense battlewagons, aircraft carriers, cruisers, troopships, supply ships, submarines, tenders, and small fry like us. We could read the future as if in a crystal ball. We were about to invade Japan.

We had hardly anchored when we were ordered back to

I try out a magician's beard in the Philippines. Wearing
beards was against navy regulations, in the event of fire
aboard ship, but the captain indulged me as long as I
kept it short.

sea in such haste that we hadn't time to refuel. One of our incoming carriers had had a torpedo shot at her.

Hours later our sonar, the underwater ears of the ship, picked up a submarine below—*ping! ping! ping!*—and we began dropping depth charges. We waited and watched. A few seconds later the explosion below reached the surface, flashing the sea white. We looked for debris, but nothing surfaced.

The darkened sonar shack was just off the bridge, and I could hear the continuous *ping! ping! ping!* echoing from below. The sub was still down there, motionless, hoping we would lose her. We made another run, rolling more depth charges off the fantail racks. Another miss. And another.

We lobbed a widening flight of hedgehogs, the rocketlike mortars. We watched the waters for black oil, for debris, for a telltale anything, even though subs were known to release oil and old clothing to fake the enemy. But nothing came bubbling up. This sub was as elusive as the floating mine we'd had such trouble shooting out of the water months before.

And then sonar lost contact. The sub was gone. Vanished.

Going by the book, we began steaming in ever-widening, concentric circles, expecting to pick up the enemy again. A sub was bad news, and we had to stop her. We depth-charged any suspicious echo from below. A large fish could unleash another drop.

A second DE joined us in the search. Another fruitless hour, and we gave it up.

When we steamed back to our base, we were so short of fuel we couldn't zigzag, a constant weaving back and forth to make ourselves a more difficult target. We steered a straight-arrow course.

Days later, on her way to join our strike force, the heavy cruiser *Indianapolis* was torpedoed. It was the last naval disaster of the war. The huge ship sank in the dark, just after midnight, with a loss of almost nine hundred men. Many of them, afloat in life jackets, were attacked by sharks.

It had happened somewhere east of the position where we'd picked up the enemy. Was it the same Japanese submarine that struck the *Indianapolis*?

It was possible. The chain of events haunted our conversations. Someone said that the Japanese had few seagoing submarines left (the scuttlebutt was true; later we learned the number: only four). Was it then the same sub we'd been depth-charging? Perhaps. Perhaps not. I don't know.

Fresh warships continued to arrive, dropping anchor in Samar Bay. Not far off, in the much broader Leyte Gulf, the navy was gathering another strike force. I got the feeling that the big invasion was only days away. The entire Pacific fleet seemed to be fueling up.

For the first time it flashed across my mind that I might become a casualty. There were going to be a lot of dead bodies. What if the DE 447 took a hit? Some of us would be killed. Me? Why not indestructible me? Aw, don't borrow trouble. If the ship sinks, swim.

I was to learn later that the military planners had made some secret calculations. They expected casualties to run to a million and a half of us farm boys and city slickers. Japanese casualties were figured at ten to fifteen million. The invasion of Japan would be a bloodbath.

And then the captain made an announcement over the intercom. "We have dropped a big new bomb on a Japanese city called Hiroshima, an atomic bomb, very powerful, very powerful. It leveled the city. The Japanese are expected to surrender."

I recall grins and smiles from my shipmates, but the news was too confounding to rate a cheer. A single bomb big enough to level a city—could this be true? We talked about it in loose knots on deck and along the passageways. What the hell was an atomic bomb? How could one bomb knock out an entire city? It sounded preposterous. I reserved judgment and went about the ship's business.

A week later the Japanese surrendered, and the war was over.

That night Samar Bay looked like the Great White Way. Every warship turned on her lights. Searchlights wagged across the sky. Signal flares were shot off and hung like descending bonfires. Everywhere running lights glowed Christmas red and green. The ship's radios, crackling with extemporaneous chatter, were turned up full blast. Aircraft guns joyously cut loose. Tracers shot blinking lights into the sky. It was a fireworks show across what must have been fifty square miles of water.

We'd be going home.

SHANGHAI

Are you rich?

We would be going home, but I couldn't pack my seabag. The DE 447 had been ordered to China.

And remember that nice day of fishing off the San Bernardino Strait? Now that the war was over, a small, barely operational Japanese submarine, lying in wait in the mouth of the strait for shipping targets, rose to the surface and surrendered. The captain must have watched us at anchor, fishing poles hanging over the side. Lucky us. We weren't a big enough ship to waste a precious torpedo on.

The DE 447 had survived some ten months of the war only to run into a typhoon on the way to China. The waves heaved and quivered and fell, the winds shrieked, and we got flung about. But we managed to keep our balance and made our way like veteran tightrope walkers. Unlike our shakedown cruise, no one got seasick. No one missed a meal. It was just another day at sea.

Later I would draw on the typhoon in a novel, *By the Great Horn Spoon!,* to describe the *Lady Wilma* encountering furious

111

seas off Tiera del Fuego at the tip of South America. A storm is a storm.

In spare moments, all the way from Panama to the South China Sea, I had been struggling to write new stories at the ship's typewriter. Having broken into *Liberty* magazine, I was able to get a literary agent in New York, Sydney Sanders, to handle my work. He tried, but not even a top agent could sell clumsy work. The sale to *Liberty* was a fluke. I was still playing "Chopsticks" on the typewriter. I'd write a story and hope I'd accidentally got things right. I was still an amateur.

Shanghai turned me into a novelist.

As we steamed up the swift, muddy Whangpoo River toward the fabled city, I caught my first sight of Chinese junks, their ribbed sails spread like great weathered fans. A drowned hog, hugely bloated, came floating along in the tide. I began to jot down notes.

We dropped anchor off the waterfront and were immediately assaulted by small bumboats offering tourist goods for sale—rice bowls and kimonos and embroidered slippers. Other boats clustered about, anxious to serve as water taxis.

I could hardly wait to go ashore. The great sophisticated city, the Paris of the Orient, as it was called, lay before me almost close enough to touch. I could hear the jingling of bells from the endless herd of bicycles and rickshas along the waterside promenade, the Bund.

For the first time I took advantage of my position as yeoman. As I made up the liberty lists, I put myself on the first section to go ashore. I changed into my whites, hailed a water taxi, and stepped ashore in China.

Within half an hour I was a millionaire.

I had no trouble finding a currency exchange, for Shanghai

had a large international population, with English, French, Russian, and German quarters. Now the city was suddenly awakened from a wartime nightmare; the long Japanese occupation was over. Those of us with the U.S. Seventh Fleet were the first Americans in years to walk along Shanghai's elegant boulevards.

I had taken my traveler's checks ashore and ripped out a few to be changed into Chinese currency. The teller did some rapid fingering on his abacus—clackety, clackety, click, click, clackety, click—and began shoving neat piles of Chinese yuan, like paper bricks, across the counter to me. By the hour inflation, running almost at the speed of light, was turning the Chinese dollar into wastepaper. I must have had a couple of million yuan.

How was I to carry it? The teller wrapped my fortune in newspaper, but I'd hardly stepped back outside when rain hit the polished streets. I rushed along until I found a luggage shop. I ducked inside and came out with my millions in a pigskin case that for years later I used to carry my magic props.

When I saw that one of the main Shanghai boulevards was evocatively named Bubbling Well Road, my enchantment with the city and with the Orient began. I accumulated copies of the English-language newspaper, the *Shanghai Evening Post and Mercury*, figuring they'd come in handy for research. I could feel in my bones that I'd found an address for a novel.

I discovered a large population of Jewish refugees who had escaped the Nazi Holocaust. Finding no safe harbor in the pious West, they had fled in the late 1930s to Shanghai, where the compassionate Chinese opened their doors. But the arriving Japanese, imitating their German partners in war, herded the Jews into a shabby ghetto in Hongkew across Soochow

Creek. This was irony from hell. It was in Hongkew that I rambled across a narrow, bar-lined street with a slang name, Blood Alley. I would use it as a book title.

I tramped the streets of Shanghai for three weeks and, with added research, got five novels of suspense out of the Far East. *Blood Alley* would be made into a major film and launch my career as a screenwriter.

A HOUSE
WITH
A VIEW

Do you live in a manchion?

When I left Shanghai, my seabag was half full of silk. With my millions of yuan I had bought an embroidered silk kimono for Betty, silk pajamas for Pearl and Honey, and silk yardage for my mother and for everyone else. I knew nothing about fabrics, but when in the silk shops the elegant stuff was only fifty cents a yard, I had a hunch I ought to bring about a mile of it home.

I had left the DE 447 anchored in the Whangpoo. You needed points, based on length of service, to qualify for discharge. I had points coming out of my ears and was one of the first to be detached to a transport home.

The DE 447 got orders for Hong Kong and French Indochina. I never saw it again. But for years I dreamed about being back aboard. I was not crazy about the war. But I had a passion for the sea.

The transport took the northern arc, the shortest route, back to the States. We steamed close enough to Alaska to catch cold, running into several days of rough, bouncy weather. A number of the big-ship sailors, off solid flattops and battlewagons the size of small countries, were turning green with seasickness. We small-ship sailors had got our sea legs riding the bucking broncos of the fleet. We regarded the transport, plowing through the storm, as steady enough to thread a needle.

To help break the monotony of the three-week crossing, a talent show was staged on the cargo deck. There's no telling what talents you may find lurking in any large group. I remember a sailor comedian doing a hat-juggling routine and a sailor tenor singing "The Road to Mandalay." And some sailor did a magician act.

I don't know how Betty discovered exactly where I'd be and managed the timing. But when I marched down the aisle for the discharge ceremony on Terminal Island near Los Angeles, there in an aisle seat she sat with a small hat clinging to her head. Dumbfounded, I gave her a quick, brush-by kiss without breaking rank or getting court-martialed. The war was really over.

We qualified for San Diego housing that was mushrooming for returning veterans, and we were lucky. For twenty-one dollars a month, we were assigned a one-bedroom bungalow on a hill overlooking Sunset Cliffs with a wide-open view of the Pacific Ocean. We could see clear to China.

We went shopping for plates and silverware and found the backseat of a car in an auto wrecking yard. I backed the seat with a used sheet of plywood, and Betty covered it with fabric. With the war effort so urgent and demanding, manufacturing for consumers had been largely put on hold. It became trendy to make a living room couch out of a used car seat. It was comfortable. We had it for years.

The war was over. On the transport carrying us back home across the northern Pacific, a talent show was organized. Here I'm doing a mind-reading trick. The challenged young warrior selected a card, unseen by me. I then paced the boxing ring attempting to pick out of the air his mental vibrations. "You're thinking of a red card, is that correct? A heart? You selected the five of hearts!"

Betty at the time we were reunited and I returned
to civilian life.

Buddy, in the army, had served out the war in Fiji. Inspired
by his success in replacing the connecting rods in our old
car a few years before, he became an airplane mechanic. His
mother was still attempting to write fiction. Sadly, she would
never see any of her work published.

I easily slipped back into civilian and family life. Pearl had
had her first child, Martin, and would soon have her second,
Carol. Honey was almost grown up and was about to be gradu-

ated from high school. Now that women were working, Ma helped Dad in his store, where her intelligence and Velcro memory were assets. Dad had moved his clothing business, enlarged to include a full line of jewelry, under the name Lewis Outfitting Company. Why Lewis? It was a backward smile to his first immigrant days, when, to avoid being taken as a greenhorn, he'd adopted the name Louie.

Instead of returning directly to college, I decided to buckle down as a full-time writer and see if I could make enough to pay the rent. Betty still had her college typewriter, a lipstick red Royal portable, and I chained myself to it. She got a job with the Veterans Administration to keep me in postage.

I wrote short stories at a furious rate. My literary agent let me go; he'd no doubt kept me on only because I was in uniform. On my own now I mailed out story after story. They'd bounce back so fast I had to duck. I'd slip each rejected tale into a fresh envelope and mail it off to another magazine.

By the following summer I was keeping fifteen to eighteen stories floating in the mails. I'd start at the top markets, the *Saturday Evening Post, Collier's,* and *Liberty,* and work my way down to the lesser fry. Now and then a story would get picked off for a few bucks—*This Week,* the Sunday newspaper supplement, and the *Toronto Star Weekly* come to mind—and we'd celebrate.

I was undaunted by the alluvial pile of printed rejection slips accumulating on my desk. (Why do apprentices keep these paper gravestones? You'd read about defiant writers who would wallpaper their offices with them.) I had been reading a new mystery novelist who turned out jeweled similes and metaphors, Raymond Chandler, and I decided to shift gears. I'd try my hand at a detective novel.

THE
STRAW
DONKEY

---

*Here's my phone number, but
please don't call collect.*

I was in a hurry. We couldn't finance too many months of
work on a novel. I didn't take time to plot a story in advance;
I jumped right into Chapter One. I had no idea where the
rush of words would take me:

> *He was a man of unusually large frame in a blue chalk-
> striped suit.*
>
> *He crossed San Diego's Fifth Street against the signal and
> turned in from the gray morning sidewalk to the Verlaine
> Building. The elevator operator was a skinny redhead with
> more lipstick than lips. "Well, Mr. Brindle," she said.
> "You're an early bird this morning."*
>
> *"I've got a date with a worm."*

Thus spake my detective, Max Brindle. He would return to
my life in a greater starring role fifty years later.

I began improvising, writing at top speed. I had read in one
of the trade magazines that a professional should be able to
write twenty pages a day, and I believed it. How I tried! When

Betty came home at end of the day, I'd grouse that I'd had a rotten day: I'd been able to write only ten or twelve or fourteen pages. Exclamation point.

At this slapdash first-draft speed, I didn't stop to find the exact right word. I'd do that later. I hadn't time to pin down missing facts or prop up sagging scenes. They could wait.

When, as the chapters stacked up, I felt the tension slacken, I'd kill off another character. That sped up things. When I saw a couple of hundred pages rising on my desk, I faced a new crisis. I'd neglected a vital detail. I didn't know who was committing all these baffling murders.

I made an amazing discovery. Of my surviving characters, I could have created a rationale for any one of them to be the guilty party. I chose the least likely villain and finished off the story.

This improvisation changed me. It gave me the brash confidence to start a novel without knowing the ending. In all the years and books since, I've never lost a novel because I couldn't figure out how to tie things up for the final curtain.

As a clue in the mystery, I'd thrown in a Mexican straw donkey, so common in the tourist stalls of Tijuana, and slapped on a title: *The Straw Donkey Case*. The book had taken two and a half weeks to write.

This first novel set some of my writing habits in cement and forever banished others. It had been absurd and damaging advice to attempt to write faster than I could think. One reaches out for the laborsaving cliché and the previously owned plot turn.

Today I regard a single page as a spectacular day's work. Sometimes I can barely sweat out a paragraph. Each writer finds his or her own composing pace. Jack London wrote *The*

Call of the Wild at a daily stint of a thousand words. I have never set myself a quota. Perhaps as a result, I have never had ulcers.

As for the traditional higgledy-piggledy first draft, I said *never* again. I didn't have a readable book. I had a 225-page trash pile.

With the creative rush spent, I found making the repairs a nightmare of tedium. I had to drag myself to the typewriter, week after dreary week. Everywhere I ran into clumsy sentences. I found whole chapters riding on their rims and in need of major overhaul. I had to chase down missing facts and do something about the Day-Glo clichés. Mark Twain said, "The difference between the right word and the almost right word is the difference between lightning and the lightning bug." I had to spray every page for vermin.

Some authors have told me they most enjoy this part of the writing process; it only goes to prove that in creative work there is no right or wrong way. There is only the way that suits you best.

I made up my mind that with the *next* book, I'd take time to get things right the first time.

The Straw Donkey Case was published in 1948 by a shabby little New York company, Phoenix Press. I don't remember why I chose this house. I have a hunch I saw a notice in one of the writer's magazines that the editor was looking for mysteries. Or I might have realized that the novel was nothing more than a finger exercise and that it would be a waste of time and postage to send it off to any of the major publishers. At any rate the editor smiled, and I received an advance of $150 against royalties.

The advance was a pittance, but the couple of months I now

had invested in the book had been validated. I pinned my hopes on the royalties to come and sat down to write another novel.

This time I rolled into the typewriter a sheet of carbon paper to make a second copy behind the top sheet. This would psych me into writing as if the first draft were the final draft, ready for the printer. I'd take my time. I'd think first and type later. I'd find the right word *now*. I'd polish each page before advancing to the next. I'd be carving in stone.

I wasn't entirely successful. I kept ripping a lot of paper out of the machine and starting again. But this revise-as-you-go way of writing is essentially the way I work today.

I write the first page once, twice, ten or twenty times before I get everything as right as I can. Only then do I move on to the second page, and the third. I used to trash reams of paper over minor changes in the text; the computer has made the whole process easier, less wasteful, and less exhausting.

With those finished, carefully wrought chapters piling up behind me, I can venture ahead into the story's unknowns. I feel like a swimmer whose toes can always touch solid bottom.

When I reach the last page, the novel is done—almost done. Inevitably I do some spot revision, trim off bits of fat, and pounce on skulking typos. I make chiropractic adjustments here and there. But the hard day labor is behind me. Nothing remains but to drop the manuscript into the mail.

I sent the second novel, a Max Brindle sequel, to Phoenix Press and was again offered a $150 advance against the royalties it would surely earn. Could Easy Street be far behind?

29

GOOD-BYE, STATE

---

*Your books are funny. Most
writers write about school or
some other boring subject.*

I was to discover an oddity in Phoenix Press's business practices: It neglected to send along royalties. You needed to yell for them. By the time I discovered that you must demand your money, Phoenix Press had gone out of business. Unlike the promise of its name, it has never risen from the ashes with my long-overdue royalties in its beak. The bird proved to be a common vulture with delusions of grandeur.

After eighteen months chained to the typewriter, two book contracts, and five short story sales, I had earned a total of $470. Betty's salary kept us going, together with the few bucks I earned with my magic act.

With the government subsidizing veterans seeking a college education, I returned to State. A writer needed all the education he or she could get, and we'd have a modest meal ticket for a while.

By that time I didn't expect any college course to turn me from a literary frog into a publishable prince, but one teacher did whisk away a few warts. I signed up for a course in the short story taught by Mr. William Brunner, a southern gentleman working on his doctorate and not yet a professor.

His past was hung with curious literary ornaments. Even English majors must make a living, and he'd gone right from graduation at the University of Virginia to the editorship of a magazine in New York, a pulp western. This was during the triumphant days of all-story magazines in flashy covers: westerns, romances, mysteries, foreign adventure. Their names ranged from *Black Mask*, where Dashiell Hammett and Raymond Chandler first published, to *Ranch Romances, Blue Book*, and *Dime Detective*. These pulps were the television of their day. All were printed on coarse wood-pulp paper that gave the genre its name. I'd submitted some of my stories to the pulps. Even *they* had rejected me.

When Mr. Brunner noticed that his harum-scarum authors were making more than he, he began writing pulps, two five-thousand-word stories a week, at a cent a word. A hundred dollars a week was then a fortune. In due time he burned out and quit the rowdy literary life to pursue his academic ambitions.

Now here was a teacher who had actually written published stories, hundreds of them. He knew the closely held secrets of the trade. He was a pro. I was in luck.

I had bought a booklet marketed to naive writers that provided hundreds of synonyms for the lowbrow, gum-chewing word *said*. He spotted something wrong at once. "I don't think you are aware, Mr. Fleischman," he opined, "that there is an invisible word in the English language."

"Invisible word?" I inquired.

"It's the word *said*," he averred. "You seem to have a passion for graceless synonyms."

125

"I won't do it anymore," I said.

It was Mr. Brunner who gave me the most useful piece of writing advice I ever received. I always pass it on.

When I told him I'd begun a new novel—a novel for children—he offered to take a look.

In due time I sat in his office as he flipped through the pages. A prematurely graying man, he looked up and fixed me with slightly aggrieved eyes. "Mr. Fleischman," he said, "there's nothing wasted but the paper."

It slowly dawned on me that the news wasn't so bad. He was telling me that the arts take *practice*. When aspiring writers send off their first work to editors, it's much like an aspiring musician sitting down to the piano one week and expecting to play Carnegie Hall the next. I'd done it. Of course I'd noticed in school that kids who could draw were always sketching things; they practiced without realizing it. And basketball players were forever shooting baskets. In the arts no one is exempt. Writers, too, must practice. Nothing is wasted but the paper.

So I was on the right track after all, for I'd stumbled on to the secret for myself. I'd been in rehearsal for years; I simply needed to hang on a bit longer. Today when I am asked for advice, I'm apt to say that the only secret to writing is that there are no secrets. "But if there were one, it could be revealed in a single word: practice. Nothing is wasted but the paper."

Pass it on.

I finished the novel and destroyed it. What did I know about writing for children?

I was twenty-nine years old on the terrifying day when State College turned me loose on the world. A few months later I became a father.

CITY
ROOM
DAYS

I'm considering being a writer.
I am getting 100s on my spelling
tests. Is that a good start?

It had taken me ten years to get a Bachelor of Arts degree. But my God, what was I going to do with it? Once a doctor is issued his scalpel, he can go to work taking out appendixes. A lawyer sues. What's an English major to do?

I'd once seen the hit play *The Front Page*, about a fast-talking Chicago newspaper reporter, Hildy Johnson, and along the way I'd taken a couple of classes in journalism. So I left my phone number and résumé at the *San Diego Daily Journal*, in the event it cared to discover another Hildy.

It was *The Straw Donkey Case* that gave me a leg up. Some three weeks later the city editor, Fred Kinne, phoned. Most newspaper reporters have unwritten novels in their hip pockets. Mine was published. Not that Fred cared to read it, but he supposed I could spell all the words. I had a job. As a copyboy.

A twenty-nine-year-old copyboy? That's the kid who runs news stories from desk to desk and fetches coffee. And at a cut in salary at that, for I'd just located a job with the city.

Fred could read my mind. "Think about it, and call me back tomorrow."

I wonder how different the direction of my life would have been if I'd declined Fred's offer. For he was really offering me a foot in the door.

I took the job. I ran copy around the city room and out to the noisy composing room, where it was set in type. On my own I dug up a couple of feature stories and handed them in. Fred published them.

Two weeks later he took the cigar out of his mouth and stopped me on my appointed rounds. "I'm putting you on the rewrite desk," he said, and turned back to his blue pencil.

For the next year I sat at a battered oak desk, phone often at my ear, with my fingers usually rattling away on the typewriter.

It was *The Front Page* with palm trees. I fielded stories from the police reporter and hammered them into prose. I went out on feature stories. I reported disasters. I covered the waterfront and flower shows. I wrote obituaries. I had to learn everything, fast and all at once.

Sap green as I was, I was accepted as a colleague by the raffish bunch of young reporters in the city room. Next to me at the bank of rewrite desks sat a tall, polished stylist, Lionel Van Deerlin. When he saw me struggling with an elusive lead for a forest fire story, he took a look and whispered the words I needed.

There was fast-moving Jack Olsen and Jerry Cohen with a unflappable Missouri drawl. Tom and Esther Gwynne became lifelong friends. Esther, too, had been made a fledgling reporter straight from State College. Tom, a second-generation San Diego sports columnist, wrote at machine-gun speed. He'd have a story finished before I could type my by-line.

Facing me across the desks sat the most celebrated man in the city room, Sanford Jarrell. Now wispy-haired but straight-backed, Sanford had committed one of the most notorious and comic hoaxes in journalism history. He's in all the books.

Then a young reporter on a major New York paper, he'd been sent out to Long Island Sound on a brisk midwinter night to look for whiskey smugglers. This was during Prohibition days, when strong spirits were illegal.

After a few hours of freezing in the bushes and unable to spy out any smugglers, Sanford found a warm speakeasy. He ordered an illegal gin and wrote a detailed and fabulous account of a fleet of cabin cruisers landing their cargo of booze along the midnight shores of the Sound.

When the story hit the street, it created a sensation. The other New York papers, not taking lightly to being scooped, sent their reporters out the following night. The newsmen froze but saw nothing. Sanford, from his warm tavern, ordered another illegal gin and wrote another account of smugglers arriving in fleet strength.

After a few more glacial nights the other reporters began to suspect fiction and made public charges of a hoax in progress. Sanford cavalierly confessed and was fired.

But his career as a fiction writer was far from over. On Saturday afternoons, when the final edition was put to bed, I'd see him roll fresh paper into the typewriter and write a thousand-word short story for the *New York Daily News*. The job never took him more than half an hour. He'd give his masterpiece a fast read and mail it off. Every week the *News* sent him a fifty-dollar check, doubling his income.

I watched his Saturday exhibition in amazement. He'd reach

into thin air for a plot. The words poured out effortlessly, every comma in place. I could never be that nimble. The stories were, of course, literary mayflies, as disposable as the daily tabloid they were written for. But I felt as if I were watching de Maupassant writing his hundreds of stories for the Paris newspapers; Sanford lacked only the genius.

My own fiction writing had been put entirely on hold; I was learning a new profession, and our daughter Jane was getting herself born.

One could have predicted that Jane would grow up to be a woman of unfailing thoughtfulness. She took care to be born on a cheerful, sunny day in April and at a most considerate and convenient hour, shortly before noon.

When I first saw Jane, it was love at first sight. I didn't mind changing her diapers. I didn't mind feeding her. I was thrilled to be a father. I still am.

At that time we had our first dog, a brilliant dachshund, Anex, and Jane wrapped her mind around him and never let go. She grew up with a passion for all living things. As a young woman with a house of her own, she discovered a population of snails where the garden should be. She collected the pesky creatures in coffee cans but was unable to kill them. In the dark of night she humanely released them in the city park.

Changes were taking place at the *Journal*. Van Deerlin took over as city editor, and I took over his political beat and began writing the political column. So it was that I was in a position to cover Richard Nixon as he wrote the manual on political dirty tricks in his first run for the U.S. Senate. I once wrote an entire column on the boneless Nixon handshake; it was like wrapping your fingers around a squid. I could hardly foresee that flashing lights and smoke bombs right out of *The*

Wizard of Oz would eventually carry this petty man to the presidency. I was getting my political education.

Late in May I got an afternoon phone call from Gene Souligny, one of the staff photographers. "Have you heard the news?"

"What news?"

"We're out of a job, Sid. The *Journal* just folded."

THE
27-INCH
MAN

I may sound normal,
but I really am different.

Even those who didn't like the brash, upstart *Journal* mourned its sudden death. San Diego would in effect become a one newspaper town. Merchants knew that without competition the Copley chain's morning and afternoon papers would be able to hike advertising rates (they did). And no longer would there be a healthy political dialogue in town; it would become a Republican monologue.

From the city room there was a rush for lifeboats. Sanford Jarrell, Jerry Cohen, and Fred Kinne found newspapers in other cities eager for their formidable talents. Lionel Van Deerlin and I decided to start a weekly newsmagazine.

It would be a pipsqueak alternate to the humorless but richly endowed papers across town. We adopted a small format, about the size of a paperback book, and gave it a pointed name: *Point*.

Joined by Jack Olsen and Bill Noonan, as staff artist, we got out the first issue in six weeks, and it was an instant hit. None of us had any business experience, a fact that surfaced a couple of weeks later, when our bills came in. While *Point*'s cover price was ten cents, it was costing us *sixteen* cents a copy to print. With almost no advertising, the success of the magazine was killing us.

By reducing the number of pages and omitting salaries, we were able to hang on. The low moment came on a week when we had only one advertiser, a Chinese restaurant, and in making up the pages, Van Deerlin forgot to put that solitary ad in the magazine. We never did get the hang of business.

Several weeks later *Point* broke a story that flashed across the country. During the *Journal*'s last weeks I had interviewed a flying saucer savant who had got his hands on a picture of an extraterrestrial who had landed on the outskirts of Mexico City. It showed a silvery twenty-seven-inch man.

The picture was so clearly faked, and the flying saucer man so clearly a dabbler in hoax and numskullery, that the *Journal* refused to run the story.

I dug out my notes, and we ran the picture of the diminutive "aluminum man" together with a tongue-in-cheek story in *Point*. It never crossed our minds that we needed to slugline or identify the craziness as fiction.

We were wrong. There were believers out there. Within hours the issue sold out on the newsstands. The 27-inch Man made national radio news. Our phone rang off the hook. Flying saucer zealots flocked to our office, begging for the historic issue. We had tapped into a tabloid audience no one knew existed until decades later, when the *National Enquirer* and the *Star* came along.

To satisfy demand, we republished the hokey-pokey photograph. The daffiness made me aware that whimsy and malarkey can't be taken for granted. After all, there are still people

Here, by demand of POINT's harassed newsstand dealers, is a reprint of the now famous photo purporting to show a 27-inch man who survived the crash of a flying disc near Mexico City. The "interplanetary" visitor, said to have died within a few hours, posthumously boosted POINT's circulation to an eight-weeks' peak for the Aug. 25 issue.

This twenty-seven-inch gent from outer space put our magazine on the map. Some people believed he was real.

who believe the world is flat and that Elvis is alive.

In the fall I learned that Fawcett Publications was launching a new line of paperback novels. To be called Gold Medal Books, they would not be the usual reprints but *original* novels. To lure authors away from their hardcover publishers, Gold Medal offered a two-thousand-dollar advance minimum, a lofty sum in 1950. As a further temptation, Fawcett would pay authors on print orders, not on copies sold. That eliminated the book-keeping and the six-month delays before royalties could be sent out.

I didn't notice that Ernest Hemingway and John Steinbeck were dropping everything to write Gold Medal novels, but a number of hungry young authors soon to be famous took the bait—among them, Louis L'Amour, John D. McDonald, and (under a pseudonym) Gore Vidal.

Since *Point* was still unable to pay salaries, Jack Olsen had already left to join *Sports Illustrated*. With a wife and child to support, I decided to give Gold Medal a try. Maybe I'd write a novel set in China.

Tom and Esther Gwynne took over my interest in *Point*, and I sat down at Betty's red Royal portable typewriter. I began a suspense story about an American newspaperman in Shang-hai. Three months later I mailed Gold Medal a novel, *The Man Who Died Laughing*.

I liked the title. Dick Carrol, the salty editor at Gold Medal, liked the novel but not the title. It was published in August 1951 as *Shanghai Flame*.

Paperbacks then sold for twenty-five cents; I was to receive a cent and a half a copy. A first edition of two hundred thousand copies was ordered from the printer, and I received three thousand dollars right off the bat. A second printing was ordered. Gold Medal sent me another check. I was filthy rich.

Betty and I talked about running off to Europe. Maybe we'd even live there for a while so that Janey would grow up bilingual.

Betty began making detailed plans while I finished a new suspense novel. This was about a nightclub magician (what else?) in Portuguese Macao, off Hong Kong, who gets involved in some gallant derring-do. This was my first experience with intense research, as I had been to neither Hong Kong nor Macao. I made notes on three-by-five index cards, and then, in moving about, I shed them like autumn leaves. I had to find a better way to organize my notes, and eventually I would.

Early the following March, Betty, Jane, and I hopped a propeller-driven plane for New Orleans, where we were to catch a freighter for Europe. *Point* was soon to be bought out by *San Diego Magazine* and sadly vanish, a playful footnote to the history of Southern California journalism. Van Deerlin was persuaded to run on the Democratic ticket for the U.S. Congress; he served in the House of Representatives for eighteen years, with distinction and irrepressible humor.

We boarded a Lykes Bros. freighter and set out to sea with one large suitcase filled with diapers and baby clothes, for we were expecting a second child. Where would it be born? Paris? Venice? Monte Carlo? We'd have several months to choose a gaudy place-name for the birth certificate.

EUROPE

---

*I suppose you want to know
all about me, so here goes.*

We landed in Genoa. Even though the war had ended almost seven years before, Europe still was pockmarked with machine-gun fire. Apartments with their front walls blown out stood like old stage sets. I wasn't in California any longer, Toto, and began making notes.

Gold Medal asked for some character revisions on the Macao novel, *Look Behind You, Lady,* and we holed up in Innsbruck, Austria. There I chained myself to the red portable for a few days while Betty poked around the town and Janey took her naps, undisturbed by the nearby rattle of the typewriter. At last the job was done, and we could get on with our travels.

In Zurich we rented a car for a month and decided that it might amuse the new baby to be born on the French Riviera. But we were so reminded of Southern California—the same squat date palms, the same red-tiled roofs, the many shades of beige—that we decided to have a look at Paris, and Paris delighted us. I'd be able to write my novels at a table in a sidewalk café.

It was at just such a table that Betty turned to me and said, "Sid, I think we should go home."

After only several weeks of gypsying around Europe? I gave her a lifted-eyebrow look. "What's wrong?"

"This pregnancy. It doesn't feel right."

"We'll get a doctor."

"Darling, I want to go home."

And so it was that Paul didn't get to be born in Paris. We sailed to New York aboard the SS *Mauritania*. With the Gold Medal check waiting for me for the Macao novel, we bought a car and drove across country, looking for a place to live.

In window-shopping for a city or town, you first see grim railroad tracks, dusty gas stations, and downtowns with interchangeable chain stores. We kept looking over the horizon, where the next town was bound to be more bewitching than the one we were just leaving. We kept driving west until we ran smack into the Pacific Ocean. Betty's sister, Dorothy, lived in a woodsy house in Pacific Grove, on Monterey Bay, and we rented a place in nearby Carmel.

Paul was born, caesarean and healthy, in September. He grew up to be a gifted writer, winning in 1989 the Newbery Award, the most distinguished prize in children's literature.

After a year or so we decided to put down roots and bought a handsome hillside lot overlooking Monterey Bay. We'd build a house, an adobe house, with plenty of room for the kids and, at last, a separate office for me.

I was dismayed when the bank turned down the ten-thousand-dollar loan we would need to build it. With my Gold Medal prospects, I saw myself as a rising pillar of the local artsy community. The bank saw me as one of the local self-deluded, hardly the equal of panhandlers, who at least had steady incomes. What if Gold Medal turned down my next book?

I yearned to prove the bank wrong. Alas, it was right. Gold Medal turned down my next book, a spy novel for which I'd scribbled European notes.

Today, when I visit the area and pass the bank, I can't resist a little smile. For the next book I wrote hit the jackpot.

BLOOD
ALLEY

---

*Do you know how much trouble
I have had trying to write this letter?
My computer has erased it three times.*

Recalling the mean street in Shanghai nicknamed Blood Alley,
I thought it would make a strong title for a book. It would
not be the only time I launched a novel solely from a title
that excited my imagination. It would happen again with *Mr.
Mysterious & Company* and *Humbug Mountain*. It hardly matters
where a writer begins.

I began improvising a Cold War story about an entire Chinese village attempting a sea escape from Communism aboard
the local ferryboat. The flight would carry my characters
through a dangerous sea passage between the Chinese main-
land and the island of Formosa (now Taiwan). I nicknamed
the passage Blood Alley.

I finished the book during the last days of Betty's third
pregnancy. Anne, who completed our family, set off alarm
bells in the middle of a February night. I rushed Betty to the
Carmel hospital, where a caesarean was performed.

Soon after we brought Anne home, I began to feel feverish:
I had the flu. Days later Anne came down with pneumonia.

140

She had to be returned to the hospital and placed in an oxygen tent. Betty, with amazing strength, sat with her hours every day. I worried from an antiseptic distance, full of guilt.

Anne bounced back nicely, and we were soon at a familiar routine of diapers, formula, and family life. During these weeks the telephone rang twice—fatefully.

A copy of the typewritten *Blood Alley* manuscript had ended up on John Wayne's desk, and his production company, Batjac, was offering me five thousand dollars for the film rights. A family of five could live bountifully for a year on a sum like that. I grabbed it.

A few nights later the phone rang a second time.

"Sid, this is Bill Wellman."

I paused. Who was Bill Wellman? Someone from the war? From school? I hadn't a clue.

"I'm going to direct *Blood Alley*," he said.

I expressed delight. I'd never heard of him, but that was only because I hadn't been paying attention. I soon learned that his silent picture *Wings* had won the first Academy Award in 1927. He had directed such classics as *Public Enemy, A Star Is Born, Beau Geste*, and *The Ox-Bow Incident*. "Wild Bill" Wellman was not just a film director; he was one of the Olympians. The next thing he said was, "How would you like to write the screenplay?"

It was lightning striking. "I'd like to," I said calmly. What did a screenplay look like?

"How soon can you hop a plane? Would tomorrow rush you?"

I was met at the quiet old Los Angeles airport by Bob Goldfarb, a film agent in a tan jacket and yellow sweater, who would be representing my writing services. We were the same age with similar navy backgrounds, although his war service had been in Mediterranean waters as the executive officer of a feisty patrol boat. That would be the beginning of a friendship and business relationship of more than forty years.

Bob Goldfarb, my film agent for the past forty years. At the time we met, he was well qualified to talk to ravens (and other forms of animal life in Hollywood), for he graduated from Cornell with a degree in zoology. So much for agent stereotypes. Any time a problem arises in my work regarding animals, I call Bob for an immediate answer. Did you know that because of the shape of their feathers, owls are able to fly soundlessly through the air?

Bob deposited me at the Beverly Hills Hotel, and before long Bill Wellman turned up to see if he could make a screenwriter of me. A graying man with distinguished matinee idol features, Wellman had a trick of collapsing one eyelid so that he looked half blind. Then he'd fix you with the other eye, a piercing blue, as he did me almost at once.

"You're not one of the Hollywood Ten, are you?" he asked. I was startled. I'd read about the clutch of screenwriters who'd been blacklisted for refusing on principle to tell an investigating committee whether or not they were Communists.

"Me?" I muttered. Was I going to have my politics stamped like a passport before coming into town? While I had a horror of dictatorships, right and left, I also detested the noisy scoundrels assaulting freedom of thought. "I'm not even one of the Hollywood Eleven," I said.

His blind eye snapped open, and he grinned. "Duke and I wondered if you might be a blacklisted writer disguised under another name."

"But why me?" Who was Duke?

"You write so visually, so cinematically, that we figured Fleischman *might* be a pseudonym. Let's go to the office."

I wrote visually? Cinematically? That was big news to me.

The Batjac offices were in a small beige office building just off Sunset Boulevard. I soon met Duke, who turned out to be John Wayne. I'd seen him in buckskins and a cowboy hat many times, but I was now seeing him in a tweed jacket and sport shirt. He was a big but agile man, amiable, soft-spoken, and well educated. I later discovered that he was a crack bridge and chess player.

I spent my days in story meetings and my nights reading screenplays to get a sense of the form and the technical jargon.

What did POV mean? Reverse shot? Jump cut? I knew nothing.

Wild Bill, who'd earned his nickname by breaking the rules, knew everything. "But don't try to direct the picture for me. Just write strong master scenes, and I'll take care of the shots."

Finally he put me back on a plane. I was going to be allowed to adapt my novel at home. A couple of hours after I returned to Monterey, I rolled paper into the typewriter and began this new career.

LIVING
UNDER AN
AVOCADO TREE

---

*Our class is studying sexism.
How come you never make
your villains women?*

I took to screenwriting as easily as I'd once learned to back-palm cards. I already knew how to sculpt a story. I only had to give my mind a quarter turn to write for the camera lens. I *did* have a visual imagination, and it began delivering interesting entrances and angles and bits of business—a rooster, for example, perched on the dusty grille of the village Rolls-Royce.

The superficial stuff I learned in an hour. You had to number the scenes so that later the film editor would be able to assemble in sequence the hundreds of strips of film. And in order for the production people to plan the shooting schedule, you needed to slugline scenes for interior or exterior settings and day or night shooting. If I were to be photographed as I sit here, the heading would read: "1. INT. SID'S STUDY—SID AT COMPUTER—NIGHT."

Hardly a big deal. But it *was* important to allow the story to unfold in a series of dramatic scenes. A novelist may describe; a film must show. Scenes, then, are the stuff movies are made of. And by lucky instinct I had always thought my fiction through in scenes. I hardly had to shift gears to write a screen-play.

I finished the draft in some six weeks and flew back to Los Angeles. I spent several days across a polished pine table from Wild Bill going over every word of the script. He gave me a graduate course in fiction writing.

Bill himself had no formal literary background. He'd been a daredevil flier during World War I and later had somehow landed in silent films. Directing picture after picture, he'd developed a superb and subtle mind for story.

"Look, kid," he said, and pried apart two sentences of the novel and showed me a strong scene hidden there, a dinner scene that ended up in the picture. The revelation forever sharpened my writer's eye.

I remember another incident some weeks later, when he was shooting *The Track of the Cat*. An actress making pancakes was to turn angrily from the stove, and he wanted her to spill a bit of batter on the hot griddle. I couldn't see why he was taking such pains to get the timing so exactly right. Later he explained it to me.

"I want to hear the sizzle of the batter, *like the hiss of a snake*, as she turns and strikes out with her spiteful line of dialogue."

That's when I learned for a lifetime that details accumulate and that no detail is unimportant.

I was in intense training for the children's books looming on my horizon. When Wild Bill insisted that every scene end with a strong curtain line, I carried this over as an effective writing habit into my novels. Unless my imagination dries up, my chapters inevitably end with the dramatic flourish of a curtain line.

A profound change of address lay in wait for me. When I

Wild Bill Wellman directing a scene in *Blood Alley*. We're on location in San Francisco Bay, doubling as the China coast. That's Lauren Bacall in the foreground, John Wayne in the background.

finished the shooting script for *Blood Alley*, Wild Bill decided he wanted me to write the screen adaptation of James Street's boy-and-dog novel *Good-bye, My Lady*. Bob Goldfarb was called in to negotiate the terms and came out of the meeting waving a long-term contract for my services.

So we bought a house a few blocks from the beach in Santa Monica, a family home shaded in the back by a giant avocado tree and with the smell of orange blossoms in the patio. I paneled an extra bedroom downstairs, turning it into an office. It was our last move. I live here still.

Blood Alley went before the cameras in San Francisco Bay, doubling as the China coast. Whenever I think of those days, a couple of memories float like driftwood to the surface.

I had written a scene in which the escaping ferryboat, needing to hide from a patrol plane, scatters its food on deck to attract thousands of nearby seagulls. In the novel the gulls successfully screen the boat.

In order to get the scene on film, the production people bought all the day-old French bread in San Francisco and scattered it over the deck. The cameras were set in place, ready to record the blinding white arrival of the seagulls.

Only a couple of confused birds showed up.

The brighter seagulls were flocking in their thousands to the ocean. Outside Golden Gate Bridge, there was a herring run.

I quickly wrote a new sequence without any wildlife in it, hiding the ferryboat under a canopy of branches, and the shooting continued.

But we came a cropper when again I needed to hide the boat, this time in a heavy fog. There wasn't a wisp of fog south of Alaska, so Batjac brought in fog-making machines.

The trouble was that the fog machines worked only too well. When the two stars, John Wayne and Lauren Bacall, began delivering their dialogue, they were drowned out by honkings from above. The movie fog had set off the San Francisco Bay foghorns.

The picture was a box-office hit and became a television perennial. Before long I was writing an original screenplay, *Lafayette Escadrille*, based on Wild Bill's own wartime experiences as a teenage American flying for France. Here were my grammar school drawings of air battles between Spads and

Fokkers brought magically to life. It was boyhood revisited, and I went at the typewriter with a passion. Alas, that wasn't enough. The picture was a flop.

I'd begun an original western called *Yellowleg* when the screenwriters went on strike, primarily to win television residuals for their work. Typewriters all over town were idled, including mine.

I was aware that our young kids didn't exactly understand what it was I did for a living. They knew I typed a lot. One afternoon I rolled paper into the machine and decided to clear up the mystery. I'd write a book just for them.

A book about what? How about a magician and his family?

I had written a *Blood Alley* sequence calling for fog, and this is the machine that made it only too well. We set off the foghorns in San Francisco Bay, drowning out the dialogue.

As I'd just finished a lot of research for the western screenplay, I set the family in covered wagon days.

A title flashed across my mind, and I typed it out. *Mr. Mysterious & Company.* Kind of intriguing. I improvised an opening: "It was a most remarkable sight. Even the hawks and buzzards sleeping in the blue Texas sky awoke in midair to glance down in wonder."

Not bad. But what were the hawks and buzzards gazing at? Could I pry those opening sentences apart and find a story? I kept typing in order to find out.

I found the story and stumbled into the wondrous world of children's books.

MR. MYSTERIOUS & COMPANY

*Man, you're so cool. I'm voting
for you! Unless you don't write
back or you're a nerd or something.*

I decided to put our own three kids into the story as Mr. Mysterious's own children. After I finished each chapter, we'd gather after dinner in the living room, and I'd read the pages to Betty, the real Jane, the real Paul, and the real Anne.

Of these family events, Paul has written in the *Horn Book*: "He could tell from our reactions if a scene had worked or if it needed work. Our opinions were asked for. I remember being proud when my suggestion that Mr. Mysterious and his family get lost turned up in the following chapter. My younger sister, a little jealous, had less success with her proposal that their family piano ought to burn down."

As a father I wanted to hear the kids laugh, and I began reaching out for funny scenes and comic villains and dialogue with flashes of humor. This novel changed me forever. It was the first sustained comic writing I had done; it fixed my style and gave me a literary voice of my own.

Once the novel was finished, the manuscript knocked

around my desk for a couple of weeks. We'd had our family fun seeing ourselves wildly rendered into fiction. But I hesitated to send the manuscript off to my book agent in New York, Willis Wing, for he was an adult. How could I ask him to read a book for kids?

Finally I mailed him *Mr. Mysterious* with a note: "I seem to have written a children's book. If you don't care to read it, I will understand. Drop it into the wastebasket."

The real Paul, the real Jane, and the real Anne, a year or so before I wrote them into the novel *Mr. Mysterious & Company*. A patio lies behind the brick wall, and my office beyond that.

Instead he sent it off to Emilie McLeod at the Atlantic Monthly Press in Boston, who read it in bed that night and accepted it the first thing in the morning.

We took the kids to their favorite drive-in restaurant, Goody-Goody's, and celebrated with hamburgers and malts. We had our dog along and ordered him a vanilla ice-cream cone.

The thought of ever writing another children's book didn't cross my mind. The screenwriters' strike ended. Marlon Brando took an option on *Yellowleg*, my western screenplay. I was back to real life.

After a year Brando dropped the option. *Mr. Mysterious & Company* was published in a bright red jacket showing Jane floating in midair. The reviews were superb. I could hardly ask for anything more.

But more was on its way. Letters began to drop through our mail slot. Letters from kids.

I was astonished. When I wrote for adults, I was lucky to receive one letter a year, and that was generally from some snorting reader who wanted to know why I had used a semicolon instead of a colon on page 147. And no one *ever* writes to a screenwriter.

But these kids were writing to tell me they'd had fun reading the novel. I was like a comedian who for the first time hears laughter from across the footlights. I was thrilled. If a child asked me three questions, I'd type out a three-page reply. Today the volume of mail is so heavy that I can manage only a couple of sentences.

My writer's lifestyle was changing. Suddenly I was being asked to fly around the country to speak at schools and libraries and conferences and to sign copies of the novel. Many years later I won the Newbery award, and in my acceptance speech I recalled a sunny moment when I was signing slips of paper for kids in a Santa Monica library. "I looked up, and there in line stood my younger daughter, Anne, age seven, with a slip of paper in her hand. She wanted my autograph, too. I knew I had arrived."

My parents loved this literary life of mine but were somewhat baffled by it, too. The wise European in Dad didn't entirely trust words as a stock-in-trade. "Sonny boy, save your *gelt*." Money.

The European stepped out more dramatically on one of Ma and Dad's trips north to Santa Monica when the kids wanted me to show off a homemade gift. I had begun to lose my hair in my thirties, and for a birthday present they had trimmed our shaggy mutt of a dog, Buster B, and glued the clippings to a piece of fabric to make me a hairpiece. I thought the toupee was hilarious. It gave me a punk pompadour decades before spiked hairdos became trendy.

Dad fixed it with a cold eye. He didn't say a word, but it was clear what he was thinking. A father was entitled to respect. *Feh*, take it away.

It was during this period that I formed a film company with a movie star, Maureen O'Hara, and her brother, Charles FitzSimons, to make *Yellowleg*. We shot the picture near Tucson, in full color on a budget of $365,000—popcorn money for a feature with a major star even in those days. We were able to pull it off by deferring salaries, as in *Point* magazine days. We hired Sam Peckinpah to direct his first theatrical feature, and he went on to a major film career.

But it was while I was on location in Arizona that I received

On location with Maureen O'Hara in Arizona to shoot my western novel and screenplay *Yellowleg*. We formed our own production company to make the film, released under the title *The Deadly Companions*. A first-magnitude star, she was gracious, intelligent, and a charming companion.

a multipage letter from Paul, age nine. I was bowled over by the ease, maturity, and richness with which he expressed himself. It was a first clue that there might be a writer unfolding in Paul.

The picture finished, I was at liberty again. It had been so much fun writing a book for kids, it occurred to me to write another one. About what?

ANATOMY
OF A
NOVEL

---

*What was the most fun you ever had
writing a book? By the Great Horn Spoon!
is the best time I ever had reading a book.*

I recalled that charmed summer when Buddy and I had taken
our magic show on the road and panned for gold in the Sierras.
Why not set a story during the California gold rush?

A boy runs off to the diggings. That would seem to be a
story idea, but it is incomplete. An idea is like a stick of wood.
About all you can do with a stick is fling it for the dog to
chase. With two sticks, however, with two ideas, you can rub
them together and create something new: fire.

I had the second idea waiting up my sleeve. A few years
earlier I had started work on a musical for a producer at Metro-
Goldwyn-Mayer. I had come up with the notion of an English
butler imported like an art object by a newly oil-rich Texas
family. I was halfway into these merry pranks when the producer left the studio, and the project curled up and died.

How about throwing the always proper and unflappable
English butler into the rough-and-tumble of the gold rush?
Now I had the second stick and began making smoke. Twelve-
year-old Jack and his family butler, Praiseworthy, would run

off, desperately hoping to strike it rich in order to—in order to what? How about to save beautiful Aunt Arabella from financial ruin?

Almost at once ideas begat notions, and notions begat scenes and incidents and sequences. Why not have Jack and Praiseworthy stow away on a ship sailing for gold rush San Francisco? Voilà! I had my opening. And could there be a romance lurking between Aunt Arabella and Praiseworthy for an ending? I'd see.

This novel changed forever some of my work methods. Realizing that I'd have to do a lot of research, I wanted to cure my persistent problems with note taking on the backs of envelopes and other easily lost scraps of paper. I tinkered together a piece of research machinery.

I ran out and bought a blank notebook. In order to organize my wildly ranging notes automatically, I divided the book into tabbed sections: "names," "words and expressions," "dress," "foods," "prices," "flora," "fauna," "incidents," "characters," "scenes," "ideas," and "miscellany."

When I discovered in my reading that a restaurant in the gold country charged a dollar for a slice of bread—two dollars buttered—I made the entry under "prices" (and used the detail in the novel).

The notebook worked. It was easy to keep within reach as I sifted through thousands of pages of gold rush material. But it was even a greater convenience during the writing stage. When I needed to dress a character, I no longer had to search through a Dumpster of random notes for some half-remembered detail. I turned to the section marked "dress," and there I'd noted that frontier San Francisco lacked skilled laundrymen and that its muddy boulevardiers sent their starched white

157

shirts by clipper ship to China for laundering. That amazing detail, too, worked its way into the novel.

With each of my novels now, when I see research ahead, I set up a research notebook. It's always at my side like a devoted dog as I write.

In addition, I started the practice of jotting down interesting names as I stumbled across them. I spend a lot of time with my characters trying on and discarding monikers. To a fiction writer a rose by any other name does not smell as sweet. Names resonate. The look and sound of a name often help me create and fix the character. I remember a rush assignment when I was collaborating with another screenwriter and I needed to introduce a new character. "What shall we call the guy?" I asked.

"For now how about Mr. X?"

I remember turning to face my collaborator and saying, "I couldn't possibly write dialogue for a character named X."

I needed to name my English butler, and the best name of all, Jeeves, was taken.

Some weekends before, we'd gone for a family drive in the San Fernando Valley. I caught a fleeting glance of a sign: Praiswater Mortuary. By the time I jotted down the name at home, I'd misremembered it. Into my "name book" I wrote "Praiseworthy."

What a happy lapse! Now, opening the book, I saw smiling at me the perfect name for my supremely able and always resourceful butler: Praiseworthy!

I have kept name books ever since.

With my head bubbling with ideas, I began Chapter One, setting the scene in Boston. Jack and Praiseworthy stow away in potato barrels aboard the *Lady Wilma*. I thought I'd get them to the California goldfields within two or three chapters. I was dead wrong.

The moment Praiseworthy pops out of his barrel, opens his mouth, and declares himself a stowaway to the captain, unexpected scenes came tumbling out of the typewriter. A villain appears. There's a storm off the tip of South America. The ship is boarded by Peruvian cats; I had a funny notion how to use them later in the story. And a sea wind carries off Praiseworthy's bowler hat, the first visible sign of character transformation in progress.

It took me *half* the novel to get Jack and Praiseworthy to the diggings. By that time the story had generated so much momentum it seemed to write itself. The shipboard villain, Cut-Eye Higgins, turns up with his neck in the hangman's rope. Jack and Praiseworthy dig him a grave and hit gold. When they lose that fortune, they strike it rich in rat-infested San Francisco auctioning Peruvian cats. And Aunt Arabella turns up looking for Jack but with melting glances at the transformed Praiseworthy.

By the Great Horn Spoon! was published at about the same time as *Yellowleg* was released under the film title *The Deadly Companions*.

The film came and vanished in a week. The novel is still in print after more than thirty years. It has been translated into a dozen languages. Disney made it into a clumsy movie, changing the title to *Bullwhip Griffin*. Scenes from the novel have been anthologized in many classroom textbooks. Paperback copies are extensively used in California schools as collateral reading during gold rush studies.

What began with a gold pan when I was sixteen was now a mother lode of its own.

ON
THE
ROAD

How's life? Pretty ratty here.

I needed to rethink. I had backed into the field of children's books, and I liked the scenery. Writing for kids was not something to be done in my spare time. It was looming up as my main work. Maybe I'd found myself at last—and I didn't know I'd been lost.

Meanwhile, invitations to speak around the country came flooding in. The immediate problem for an author, I quickly discovered, was how to break the ice with an auditorium full of kids. They have been primed for your visit and sit as awed as if you were Shakespeare.

Book illustrators have it easy. They almost always set up an easel and draw pictures, and kids are mesmerized. What is an author to do? Open a laptop computer and show how slowly he or she writes?

I had at my fingertips a natural icebreaker. I'd do a magic trick.

So moments after I'm introduced, I say, "I'd like to saw someone in two—if I can get anyone to volunteer."

Instantly almost every hand in the auditorium shoots up and waves to catch my attention. The formality of the occasion is broken, and the kids are themselves, yelling and eager. It's not that they're willing to risk their necks for a moment in the spotlight; they're confident that I'm not going to hurt them. But when I have used this opening before adults, usually teachers and librarians, they're not so trusting. Rarely does a single hand go up, and I have to coax someone onstage.

Spying the arms waving about, I almost never choose the most eager kid. I want to give a moment of school fame to a shy child timidly raising an arm because everyone else is doing it. Only once through the years did I have a child grow frightened on the stage and, despite my reassuring whispers, want off.

"I couldn't pack my big magician's saw," I explain. "I'll saw you in half with this." I unroll a wide red ribbon. "You'll notice it's red. In the event there's any blood, it won't show on this, and you won't faint." First big laugh.

I draw the ribbon around the volunteer and prepare to snap it through the child—visibly. At the very last moment I interrupt myself.

"I remember saying quite clearly that I would saw you in half. Did anyone hear me say I'd put you back together again?"

This line brings down the house.

Finally, at a signal, I have the kids yell out "abracadabra," the ribbon passes through the child, there's an audible gasp of stupefaction—and the kids and I are friends.

They feel comfortable enough to ask personal questions during the Q & A session.

A common one: "How much money do you make?"

I generally quip, "Not nearly enough," but use the question to explain how authors are paid with a sum in advance against sales and a royalty or percentage based on each copy sold.

"How old are you?"

I now answer, "I'm a hundred and nine years old. I just look young for my age." They go along with the gag and attempt to nag the number out of me.

Geographical area sometimes informs a question. Only in Beverly Hills would a child ask, and one did, "Who's your agent?"

The strangest question I ever had to field turned up in a rural school where a husky fourth grader asked, "Do you write Bibles?"

I was stopped cold. But I recovered quickly, for by that time I'd had enough speaking experience to realize what he was asking. Young kids often assume that the author has made every copy of his or her book. He was asking, I'm sure, whether I write, make, *publish* Bibles.

There occurred a moment of teacher quick wit when I was speaking in a Texas school and a child in the second row threw up. Instead of accompanying him up the aisle where the entire student body would see who had disgraced himself, this brilliant teacher had the entire class rise and file out, nicely camouflaging the mortified kid.

Within a few years I was spending about ten weeks a year on the road. It was something like my early days of one-night stands. I'd hop a plane and skid to a stop anywhere from Little Rock, Arkansas, to Juneau, Alaska. I'd saw someone in half, give my talk, catch another plane, and vanish. It all had an air of vaudeville, and I loved it.

Meanwhile, I had kids growing up at home. The house

The house in Santa Monica where our kids grew up and all
of my children's books have been written. This one, too.

sounded like a rehearsal room for Carnegie Hall. Jane and
Anne were practicing the flute, and Paul was on the piano. I
had undertaken the impossible, the classical guitar. Betty, an
exquisite pianist from early childhood, accompanied us all.
Home was full of grace notes.

VILLAINS
I HAVE
LOVED

---

*My favorite character is Hold-Your-Nose-Billy
because he smells like garlic and my mother
eats garlic on bread and she smells too.*

I have had a life without villains. But it's been fun creating them. I write villains cut to an uncommon pattern. My rogues wear fright wigs, but they also wear putty noses and slap shoes. They are comic villains with a hearty appetite for chewing up the scenery.

I found the model when I was writing *The Ghost in the Noonday Sun*, a story that grew out of a folklore belief. I'd tripped over an old notion that one born at the stroke of midnight has the power to see ghosts. What, I wondered, if pirates had buried treasure, had thrown into the same pit their murdered leader, but then (given my taste in villains) had lost the map? Again according to folk belief, the murdered man would pace his gravesite until avenged. Now I had something! The returning band of pirates would need someone able to see ghosts and to point out where to dig. Enter my young hero, Oliver Finch, born at the stroke of midnight.

Now that I had a Roman candle of an idea for a novel and a unique young hero, I began creating a pirate villain. In my research book I found a nickname for the devil, Old Scratch.

And Captain Scratch was born. I lit his rain-soaked entrance with a foreboding and dissonant simile. "Captain Scratch ripped open the buttons of his greatcoat and squeezed the rain out of his flaming beard as if he were wringing a chicken's neck."

By the end of the novel I'd grown so fond of the swashbuckling mariner that I couldn't bring myself to run him through with a cardboard saber. In the final island scene, awakening from a blow on the head from a falling coconut, he is stupefied to find himself rising from his own grave, headstone and all. His shipmates are persuading him that he's invisible—a wispy phantom, in fact, with the smell of brimstone rising with him from his grave. He's the ghost in the noonday sun.

This was the only novel for which I had the ending firmly in mind from the beginning, but this rattlebones scene wasn't it. I thought I was going to finish with a great sea battle between the pirate ship and a whaling ship armed only with harpoons and commanded by Oliver's father, sailing to the rescue. But when the scene arose turning Captain Scratch into a ghost, I knew the novel was finished. The sea battle would have been an anticlimax, and I discarded it without a second glance.

When Peter Sellers played Captain Scratch in the film version, he put on such a heavy Irish brogue that he needed subtitles. There was discord on the set so that like Richard III, the movie was "deform'd . . . scarce half made up," and never released in theaters. It was consigned as junk to the video stores.

Several months ago I had a letter complaining that all of my villains were men. How about making women the bad guys?

I'm not *entirely* guilty. One of my most unspeakable and harum-scarum villains is Mrs. Daggatt, who runs the orphan house in *Jingo Django*. I wrote her as every child's windy nightmare, the black widow spider of the novel. She gets what's coming to her at the end when attacked by an avenging swarm of hornets.

One of my favorite villains is Step-and-a-Half Jackson in *Me and the Man on the Moon-Eyed Horse*. Says he: "There's so many of us Jacksons in hell, ma'am, our feet are sticking out the windows."

But I suppose my most enduring villain will be Hold-Your-Nose Billy, the smelly highwayman in *The Whipping Boy*. He'd earned his sobriquet by munching garlic like radishes and had had street ballads written about him.

> *Hold-Your-Nose Billy, a wild man is he,*
> *Hang him from a gallows tree.*
> *Here he comes, there he goes:*
> *Don't forget to hold your nose.*

Once I started putting him on paper, the ignorant scalawag wrote his own lines and even seemed to mastermind his own ending. Stowing away, he makes a bad choice of ships. The vessel lifts anchor with a cargo of prisoners, off to a distant convict island.

While I was dedicating most of my time to children's books, I hadn't entirely turned my back on the adult world. After writing five scripts for Wild Bill, I broke with him and sailed off on my own.

I found it to be a refreshment to turn from a novel to a screenplay, for a screenplay is so much less demanding. You give a few clues, and the art director designs the sets, the set dresser selects the furnishings, the costume designer dresses the characters, and the actors throw in expressions and subtle inflections. Finally the director snaps the whip over all of these activities. You get lots of help.

But writing a novel is a one-person job. You design the sets; you put lamps in the rooms and pictures on the walls; you dress the actors and describe their fleeting expressions. You are the ringmaster and all the acts, and you sweep up at night.

I began a novel, but with the story barely launched I was interrupted for several months by movie work.

With the film sale of *The Ghost in the Noonday Sun* I gained a fleeting reputation as the pirate writer in town. Universal had what it regarded as a great title for a buccaneer movie

Honey, Pearl, and I, grown up at last.

and hired me to write a screenplay to support it. The film was never made. I stayed on to do some story doctoring on other scripts (uncredited) and returned to the novel that had been put aside.

By this time my writing habits were set. I'd roll out of bed in the morning, pause to warm up a cup of last night's coffee (I'd learned to drink the stuff), and invade my corner office on the ground floor.

I was no longer having any trouble facing the typewriter. Some writers sharpen jars of pencils, answer mail, work crossword puzzles, or contemplate suicide—do anything to put off the bungee jump into the day's writing stint. I came to know one writer with so many anxiety rituals that he'd rarely settle down to work before four in the afternoon.

But through the years I'd made a writing habit, so that it was as natural for me to face the blank page in the morning as it was to brush my teeth. And as I've already confessed, not knowing what was going to happen next in the story acted as a magnetic force drawing me back to my desk in order to find out.

But the story is cold in the morning, and you often need a jump start. I sometimes resort to the writer's trick of quitting in mid-sentence. In the morning the next words are in your fingertips and come clacking out, and you're off and running again.

In his last years Hemingway, we're told, used to reread his novel in progress from the very first page before he was able to scratch out the next sentences. I find it enough to polish the previous day's page or two, by which time I'm deep into the story.

I try never to quit for the day with a scene left in knots.

Facing the tangle when I'm cold the next morning will be like turning onto a country road with four flat tires. If possible, I try to cure the day's story riddles before I shut down and sharpen pencils.

At any rate, after so much film work, it was refreshing to be sitting down each morning at a novel. I had a villain named Colonel Plugg beginning to snort and carry on. What I didn't see coming was a character about to step into the spotlight and become world-famous as the hero of ten books. His name was McBroom.

ENTER, LAUGHING

Why are there so many words?

Like a case of surrogate motherhood, Josh McBroom got himself created in another book.

I had a vivid memory of a barefoot boy in a straw hat, a fishing pole across his shoulder, as he ambled down a country road. He looked at me in full color on a barbershop calendar as I, his own age, was having my hair cut.

I envied him. He lived in the country with fishing holes and unfamiliar trees to climb and wild paths to follow. I was a city kid. I'd never been fishing, and nobody climbs a palm tree.

And so I had launched a new novel on this frozen memory. *Chancy and the Grand Rascal* opens with that classic calendar picture. But instead of carrying a fishing pole, my barefoot hero is pushing a wheelbarrow. And I added, to begin opening up a plot, "His travels had begun."

A great deal of story writing is problem solving. Chancy's travels to where? And why? And what's in the wheelbarrow?

In finding the answers, I found the plot. One by one my company of actors began to emerge from the darkness, and scenes began to pop up. Almost too skinny to cast a shadow, Chancy sets out with his belongings to track down his younger sisters and brother, separated after the death of their parents. Chancy discovers that he is being followed by Will Buckthorn, the grand rascal of the story.

It was at this point in shaping the novel that McBroom began to stir. I needed a friendly battle of wits between the grand rascal and the captain of a river raft and decided on a liars' contest.

Recalling old Professor Fait's air in telling the tall tale about the delicately balanced canoe, I devised a lie about a farmer on a one-acre farm with earth so rich he could plant and harvest three crops a day. Corn grew so fast that if the farmer didn't jump out of the way when planting the seed, the stalks would skin his nose.

With the liars' contest on paper, I moved on with the story. As the characters advanced, I kept taking backward glances. I'd laughed out loud at the farmer. He didn't yet have a name, and his tale was only three-quarters of a page long. I began to wonder if I could do more with it. Maybe this pollywog could turn into a frog.

One day I simply stopped writing *Chancy* to put the farmer through the typewriter again to see what would happen. He came out with a name, a wife and kids, and a villainous adversary named Heck Jones, whose own land was so pickax-hard he had to plant seeds with a shotgun. The tall tale had grown to fifteen typewritten pages. The story was published as *McBroom Tells the Truth*.

The story was a freak happening, a one-shot. I didn't sense that there could be a series in it. I figured my modest farm epic would have the life expectancy of poster paint. I was wrong. McBroom had staying power. He made kids laugh out loud.

The following year I decided to see if there was another story in him. I decided to deal with a big wind that hits the farm, a wind so almighty strong that it sucks the McBroom children out the chimney and away—all eleven of them, Will*jill*hester*chester*peter*polly*tim*tom*mary*larry*andlittle*clarinda*.

I'm commonly asked why I ran the names together. It was part memory. I recalled from childhood the neighborhood mothers on their back porches giving a yell for their kids— one that traveled for miles. I remembered in particular the voice of my aunt Sarah. "Seymourjackeeraaalpheee! Dinner!"

That memory solved a technical problem. In a short story I had no space to define eleven separate kids. My solution was to write them as a single character. And that proved to be a happy solution, for I have learned of classroom stopwatch contests to see who can rip out the names the fastest and of the lilting names being set to music with sand block and triangle accompaniment.

I was discovering very quickly that tall tales aren't nonsense. They are superbly logical. The common details of everyday life must be left firmly in place. Like classic fantasy, comic fantasy has its taproot in the real world. But it is reality touched with anarchy. It is reality on laughing gas.

When the temperature drops enough, water freezes. Why not words? Ghost story! The McBrooms hear creaking doors and disembodied voices and believe there's a ghost in the house! But the haunted voices prove to be sounds frozen the frigid winter before, now thawing in the spring. The science is almost above reproach.

172

Again, the McBroom kids build an automobile that is both logical and fantastical. It runs on popcorn.

How perfectly reasonable! The internal-combustion engine gets its power from exploding droplets of gasoline. The McBrooms' Popcornmobile gets its power from exploding kernels of maize. Out of the exhaust pipe comes fluffy white popcorn.

Only a numskull cow would mistake the stuff for snow and freeze to death. "I did tell a lie once," adds the ever-truthful Josh McBroom. "That cow . . . didn't really freeze to death in all that popcorn. But she did catch a terrible cold."

Kids, eager to help, fill my mailbox with ideas for new McBroom stories. They would like to see me take McBroom into outer space. More down-to-earth is a girl in Michigan who suggested: "McBroom Loses His Drawers." A lightbulb idea that turns up with some frequency is "The McBrooms Go to McDonald's," almost always followed by the line "You take it from there."

By the time I'd wrapped up the McBroom sagas some eighteen years later, I'd discovered that writing comedy was easy. All you needed to start was a prodigiously funny idea. And then all you had to do was work out the hilarious possibilities.

FOOTSTEPS

I'd like to be a writer,
but my hand gets tired.
Can you give me some advice?

One by one the kids were leaving home for college, Janey to Santa Barbara, Paul to Berkeley, and Anne to Davis. Suddenly Betty and I were rattling around this big house, abandoned, alone. We developed withdrawal symptoms. When it came to the kids I'd always had a talent for worry. Now I developed a genius for it. Betty embraced pottery making. The quiet in the house was going to take some getting used to.

Now I wonder how I got so much writing done in the midst of the family three-ring circus. Fresh from school, the kids would burst into my office, often catching me in mid-sentence, to announce, "Daddy, I'm home!" I remember an occasion when Betty commanded me to abandon my typewriter. She needed the machine to address some urgent cards for the PTA.

Our social life had been changing. I was still seeing my old magician friends, but we were now meeting people whose lives, like mine, were focused on children's books. Thirty seconds after first shaking hands with Don Freeman, the big, smiling creator of *Corduroy*, I felt that I'd found an old friend.

We'd grown up a few blocks from each other in San Diego and gone to the same grammar school!

I remember an occasion when Don and his wife, Lydia, and Betty and I spent a couple of weeks together in London. We were just checking out of a restaurant in Soho when a waiter with a frayed walrus mustache caught Don's artist's eye. With his sketchbook open, Don spoke to the waiter like a general about to take prisoners. "Don't move!" Utterly baffled, the waiter froze, balancing a tray of dirty plates and wineglasses on one palm. Within seconds Don had his lightning sketch,

Don Freeman in his Santa Barbara studio. When Don was finishing a book, he would hide away from the world in a hotel or motel room. Only his wife, Lydia, would know where he was.

the waiter was immortalized, and we left. Don had a streak of the paparazzi in him.

On my frequent trips to New York I'd pal around with author-illustrator Ezra Jack Keats. Soon to win herself a Newbery, Ellen Raskin and I made a ritual of meeting for breakfast. Dinner was almost always with that dearest of women Esther Hautzig, author of *The Endless Steppe*, or that other charmer Susan Hirschman, who was to become my editor.

In and out of our house came Maurice Sendak and Clyde Robert Bulla and Julia Cunningham and Bill Peet and the poet Myra Cohn Livingston. This literary company was to have an effect on Paul.

One Christmas vacation he returned from college, and I heard him typing away in his upstairs room. Just before dinner he came downstairs and tossed a few typed pages on the couch. "I've written a story, Daddy, if you want to read it."

Of course I wanted to read it! "I didn't know you've been writing stories," I said.

"I haven't. This is the first."

I'd read many amateur stories, and the blissful lack of know-how usually reveals itself with the first page, if not the first sentence. I once read a story in which the author introduced nine characters in the opening paragraph.

I read Paul's story with growing amazement. The usual trips and falls weren't there. The story, about the bond between a boy and the tree planted to celebrate his birth, was skillfully managed and handsomely written.

Once *The Birthday Tree* was published by Harper & Row, friends and strangers assumed I had guided Paul's hand. It was not at all true. The one writer's secret I had felt obliged to show him was how to tease out an important scene for dramatic effect (stay with me; I'll return to this). Paul appeared to have instinctively known all the other "secrets." How could this be?

The answer came to me: those writers in our house, forever talking over their story problems. Growing kids have their ears open. Paul knew about denouement and the horror of flashbacks at a time when he was still reading cereal boxes.

At this time in my speeches around the country I added a few brief pointers to those in the auditorium interested in writing stories of their own. They were a captive audience; you of course may skip out unseen. In addition to tips I have dropped along the way, these have formed the undercoating to my fiction.

1. It's the job of the hero or heroine to solve the story problem; don't leave it to a second-banana character like Uncle Harry. You'd know something was wrong if Watson solved the crime instead of Sherlock Holmes. This clunky plotting sank many of my stories when I started out.

2. The main character should be changed by the events of the story. Remember your fairy tales? Change is built into the refrain at the end: "And they lived happily ever after."

3. If there's a hole in your story, point it out and the hole will disappear. For example, in *McBroom's Zoo* I wanted to use the Hidebehind, a fabled frontier creature. No one knows what the Hidebehind looks like because every time you look, the animal hides behind you.

I saw the hole at once. All McBroom needed to do was hold up a mirror and he'd see the Hidebehind's mug. I plugged the hole by pointing to it. Works like magic. "I even tried walking around with a hand mirror," McBroom declares, "but the Hidebehind was too eternal clever for tricks like that."

4. Dramatize important scenes; narrate the trivialities. I have seen a lot of this the other way around.

5. Give weather reports. It helps the reality of a scene if foghorns are blowing or kites are in the sky on a windy afternoon or the day's so hot wallpaper is peeling off the walls.

6. The stronger the villain—or opposing force—the stronger the hero or heroine. A wimpy problem delivers a wimpy story.

7. When possible, give important characters an "entrance." That's why grand staircases were invented.

8. Write in scenes. It's generally hard to find any pulse in straight narration. Color it gray. Show; don't tell. Color it splashy.

9. Imagery is powerful shorthand. It says in four or five words what might otherwise take you sentences to describe—and not as vividly. It takes time to think out fresh similes and metaphors, and they must be *apt* and *exact*. Practice helps. After a while you develop a knack for it. Clumsy imagery must be ripped up instantly.

10. If you're stuck on the plot, look around for the second stick. When I discovered a tricksy Teutonic wood spirit who turned hay into horses, I couldn't figure out what to do with it. Then I came across a Yiddish saying: "It's easier to guard a sack of fleas than a young girl in love." After I burst out laughing, the image of guarding a sack of fleas caught my fancy. The spirit could turn a guarded sack

of gold pieces into a guarded sack of fleas. *The Hey Hey Man* followed, with the elfin pixie making a return appearance in *The Midnight Horse*.

11. Don't make a mossy rock or a frying pan the hero or heroine. Stories are tough enough to write without adding to the difficulties with an inanimate object in the lead. This sort of thing is best left to the professionals, who rarely touch it.

12. Tease out important information to dramatize important scenes. Here are two versions of a phone call.

"Aunt Amanda! You just won the lottery!"

Here's the same scene, teased out. "Aunt Amanda! There's big news! I've been trying to reach you for an hour! Don't you ever answer your phone?"

"I thought it must be Gertrude calling."

"Gertrude's been dead for ten years."

"What?"

"Turn up your hearing aid."

"Why are you yelling?"

"There's wonderful news!"

"You're going to get married?"

"I *am* married, Aunt Amanda. You remember that lottery ticket you bought? I hope you didn't misplace it."

"Of course I didn't misplace it. I threw it away. I never win."

"Go through your trash, Aunt Amanda! You won! You won the lottery!"

HELLO,
MR. NEWBERY

I like Jemmy.
He's my kind of ratcatcher.

After writing for an hour or so first thing in the morning, I take a break. I shower, shave around my beard, and get something to eat before returning to my desk.

On a January morning in 1987 I stepped out of the shower, and Betty said, "You had a call from Chicago. A woman named Trev Jones."

I didn't recognize the name. "What did she want?"

"She wanted to know how long it takes you to shower."

Of the momentous news waiting for me in Chicago, I would write in the *Horn Book Magazine*: "I wandered downstairs to my office, returned the call, and heard a voice as bubbly as champagne ring out the news. A book I had struggled with for almost ten years had won the Newbery Medal.

"I don't happen to believe in levitation, unless it's done with mirrors, but for the next few days I had to load my pockets with ballast. The Newbery Medal is an enchantment.

It's bliss. . . . And it set up a Pavlovian reaction. Every time I take a shower, I expect the phone to ring."

The book was *The Whipping Boy*, a galloping tale of a ratcatcher's son whisked off the cobbled streets to serve as whipping boy to a rotten royal, suitably nicknamed Prince Brat.

The idea for the book was classic serendipity. Some years before, in researching for a different novel, I had caught sight of the origin of the term. There *had* been live and kicking whipping boys kept in royal palaces to suffer the punishments for misbehaving princes. There had been, as well, whipping girls for princesses.

At this point I made a grave error. I saw a picture book in it, and for years that's what I tried to make of the material. Only when I finally woke up and realized that I needed the elbowroom of a novel, did Jemmy, the ratcatcher's son, come to life.

I spent about three weeks writing, rewriting, and polishing a Newbery acceptance speech for the June banquet in San Francisco. And then, as I didn't care to wear secondhand clothing for the occasion, I bought a tuxedo, a cummerbund, and patent leather shoes.

I felt like a million. I was aware of gulpy anxieties as the night approached, but the moment I stepped into the spotlight, it was vaudeville all over again. I was utterly relaxed and sailed through the words. I could make out my family in the half darkness, and Susan, my wonder editor, and friends laughing at my lines as if I'd brought my own claque. I finished to a burst of applause and immediately felt as airy as a party balloon cut loose. The sensation lasted for the rest of the year.

But finally, with the last congratulatory letter answered

THE WHIPPING BOY

~~THE King was holding a FEAST.~~ ~~The young prince~~
~~while everyone was busy~~ And his son, the young
prince, was

The king ~~was~~ WAS holding a great ~~feast~~ **banquet**. ~~Everyone~~
~~was so busy eating~~ while the lords ~~who~~ were
~~banqueting~~ the young prince snuck and held
the forks and knives and tied their powdered wigs to
the backs of the chairs.

When they stood up to toast the king, there
wigs ~~were~~ flew off.

"HEE-HEE, HaHaHaw" ~~the young prince laughed~~

The young prince, hiding ~~behind a~~ behind a
suit of armor, ~~tried to keep~~ keep laughing. But ~~it burst~~
~~of~~ it ~~rolled~~ out it ripped.

"HEE-HEE, HaHaHa, Ha-Ha!" ~~he burst out~~

The king spied him, and gave an angry shout.
"Fetch the whipping boy."

The call echoed through the castle halls,
the stone stairway and finally reached a small chamber in the tower.
An orphan boy named James lay asleep. A gua...
~~and~~ his awoke

"~~Youre wanted in the great hall~~, LAD," ~~said the~~

James, the whipping boy, gave a ~~big~~ quiet such a yell,
he woke, "~~but the~~ queen do this thing?" Quickly he pulled on his velvet
breeches, his stockings and buckled shoes.

In the great hall, the king said "Twenty ~~blows~~ **WHACKS**,

The whipping boy was bent across the arm of a
chair and given a spanking of 20 blows.

Then the king turned to prince Gloffen and
said, "And let that be a lesson to you, sir!"

The earliest attempt to get *The Whipping Boy* on paper.
I couldn't find a name for the prince that seemed right.
In the second paragraph I tried Geoffrey but crossed
it out in favor of Harry, which I abandoned a few
paragraphs later. At the upper left I tried Geoffrey the
Just Awful, Thomas the Terrible, and even Kickworthy.
Eventually I found the perfect name: Prince Brat. At upper
right I have jotted down a line I wanted to be sure to use:
so mad "I could spit ink." It's quite unusual for me to
write by hand. My typewriter must have been in the shop
for repairs.

and the last phone call returned, I had to face the Newbery
syndrome. How can you possibly write again with Newbery
judges watching over your shoulder? Your sentences must be
spun out of gold.

I held my breath and took the plunge. I'd found a word
that I fell in love with: scarebird. It's only a folksy name for
a scarecrow, but for me there was a different poetry in the
look and sound of it.

I started a story about a lonely old man who begins to take
pity on the scarebird standing out in the sun and puts his old
farmer's hat on its head. When winds come along, plucking
straw from the scarebird's cuffs, Lonesome John puts old work
gloves and shoes on his silent friend, and then his yellow
raincoat against a rising storm.

At this point I didn't know where to go with the story. After
a few days of knocking my head against the wall, the missing
piece came to me. When a young man comes along looking
for work, Lonesome John resists having his solitary life dis-

turbed. But he strips off the scarebird's gloves for Sam to wear when grubbing out weeds. As needs arise, bit by bit he disrobes the straw figure, hat, shoes, and coat. The scarebird is transformed into his friend Sam.

The tale haunted reviewers. I don't get any better than *The Scarebird*.

I was syndrome cured.

CURTAIN
LINES

Are you anything like
Lonesome John
in The Scarebird?

Two years later Paul won the Newbery Award for *Joyful Noise*, and it was cartwheels all over again in Dallas. As I write this, his twentieth published book has landed on my desk. He's a father himself these days, with two boys, Seth and Dana.

Anne went on to graduate school for a master's degree in nutrition. With two young children, Zachary and Jenna, she teaches part-time at a junior college.

After graduation Janey spent several years elbow deep in nature up in the California hills in a fire lookout tower. With an equal passion for books, she now works in a public library.

I disliked writing obituaries when I was on the newspaper, and I don't like to write them now. I think there is something wrong with the lofty scheme of things. After a lifetime of work, one should be rewarded with superb health in order to have a ball in old age.

My father never missed a day's work in his life. He rejected the entire notion of illness. Running a fever, he'd dress and drive to his store and put in a full day.

It was only after he retired and should have been free to travel, perhaps with a visit to the old country, that he was felled. He ruptured his esophagus. Despite surgeries, he could get food down only in sparrow-size bits.

The wedding of his granddaughter and my niece, Carol, lay ahead, and he put on a tux for the gala occasion. He could hardly eat, but when I saw him gazing around at the assemblage in the ballroom of the Hotel Del Coronado, he must have felt that his immigrant life had been a success beyond his wildest Olik dreams. He had played a patriarchal role in the lives of so many he saw dancing around this festive room. He died a few weeks later. My mother, her hair Gypsy black and her mind sharp to the end, lived on for another ten years.

Pearl is the only member of our large family to develop that most savage of diseases, Alzheimer's. It's baffling. Why her? As I was in the midst of writing about her in these pages, she passed away.

My magic pal Buddy Ryan had been a smoker since the age of thirteen. He liked blowing smoke out through his nose. He died in mid-life with cancer of the sinus. Several of my close magic friends from those adolescent golden years have vanished, and I'm reminded of them constantly: Haskell, Bob Gunther, and Jim Conley.

The decade of the nineties blew in with a lot of film work. I adapted *The Whipping Boy* for the screen and then took my name off the screenplay. I didn't like changes made in the shooting script and chose as a pseudonym the lead character from that first mystery novel I wrote, Max Brindle. Remember him?

The family in a reunion around a favorite Santa Monica
tree. On the left and up front stand Paul; his wife, Becky; Jane;
Anne and her husband, Chad. Highest on the tree stand
Paul and Becky's boys, Seth and Dana, followed by Anne
and Chad's kids, Zachary and Jenna.

Once I'd taken my name off the screenplay, you can guess what happened. The picture got the best reviews of any film I have ever been involved with. It was released in the U.S. on the Disney Channel and won the Emmy of the cable television world, the Ace Award.

It was during this time that Betty died.

GHOST
STORY

I read Mr. Mysterious & Company,
*which my mom read
in fifth grade 32 years ago!*

I don't believe in ghosts. They're a wonderful fantasy. I've had fun with the see-through gentry in several of my books. But having lost Betty to cancer, I can understand the impulse to conjure up a familiar spirit in a billowy curtain or a breeze touching the neck.

I buried myself in a novel. We had discovered, many years before, that Betty was descended from Mary Parsons, a woman tried as a witch in Northampton, Massachusetts, in 1675.

But I remembered all those buckle-shoe Puritans in my schoolbooks and figured there wasn't a laugh to be had in early New England. For years I ducked the novel. Anyway, I didn't know where to take a bite out of the material. The Salem witchcraft trials? They'd been done many times before.

I'd always found superstitions and folk beliefs to be a rich stewpot of story ideas. Born at midnight? You can see ghosts. Or tell time by reading a cat's eyes. My favorite scene in *Chancy and the Grand Rascal* arose from that folksy bit. The

Postimpressionist artist Chaim Soutine was haunted by the superstition that we are born to speak a fated, exact number of words and keel over dead when we utter the last syllable. That moon-headed notion is at the center of *Longbeard the Wizard*.

I'd been thinking more and more about the absurdities of superstitious belief: ghosts, evil eyes, tea leaf reading, the number thirteen, crystal balls, and other claptraperies.

The number thirteen. Everyone seems to be a little fearful of that number. There is even a word for it: *triskaidekaphobia*. Santa Monica has no Thirteenth Street. I'd never been in a building with a thirteenth floor. Of course not; there'd be a spookiness there, a magic. The numbering, I knew, inevitably jumps from the twelfth to the fourteenth floor.

An idea struck like an earthquake, followed almost at once by an aftershock, a second idea. I saw a way of dealing with Betty's great-great-something-or-other-grandmother.

Say a modern kid stumbles into the magic of a thirteenth floor. He could be transported back in time to the witchcraft trial of his own ancestor. That meant everyone he met would be dead; he would be among ghosts. I could give the novel point by dramatizing the buzz-fly presence in our own times of medieval illusions and delusions—the fortune-telling parlors that still abound, the belief in evil eyes and ghosts and witches.

Now the aftershock. What if Betty's ancestor had been a child? Had kids been victims of the witchcraft trials of the seventeenth century? I held my breath and reached for an old friend on my shelves, Charles Mackay's *Extraordinary Popular Delusions and the Madness of Crowds*. It was there. Kids *had* been accused of witchcraft. Dogs, too.

I set up a research book marked "The 13th Floor" and

plowed into the first chapter. When I discovered that the age of piracy overlapped the seventeenth-century witchcraft mania, I couldn't resist bringing back my cast of rascals from *The Ghost in the Noonday Sun*. The thirteenth floor delivers Buddy Stebbins, my young hero, into the dark hold of a storm-tossed pirate ship, the *Laughing Mermaid*. In due time Captain Scratch, last seen rising in the noonday sun from his makeshift grave, makes a cameo appearance, biting off a tasty chunk of scenery.

Before long I *was* finding laughs with those buckle-shoe New Englanders. Toward the end I scared the daylights out of the thundering villain by getting a codfish to talk.

I remember, during those ancient days when I was first starting out, discovering a picture of Jack London, author of *The Call of the Wild*. My eyes roved over every detail of the room he was writing in: the stack of wire paper baskets on his desk, the lampshade, the crabby-looking typewriter, the gray light pressing through the windows. For years I kept a stack of wire paper baskets on my desk.

My desk for the past forty years is really a table, an acre of varnished pine originally custom-made for John Wayne. It's been a mess for forty years. My manuscripts, however, are compulsively neat and clean. You could eat off them.

My office is a large cypress-paneled room, with an adjoining alcove. Three walls are lined with books. In used-book shops I drag home any tome I think might be useful. Bringing up swine and cattle? I couldn't let that treasure get away. I've another on the language of the Pitcairn islanders. I may never open the covers, but what if I should need to have a character from Pitcairn speak? I might never be able to track down

My office and alcove hours after the 1994 Los Angeles earthquake. The force was directional, striking from left to right in this picture. Books on the south walls were barely affected.

that obscure book. I have shelves on the West, on piracy, on folklore, and whole bookcases on magic.

When the Los Angeles earthquake struck in 1994, Santa Monica was shaken as if inside a cement mixer. So many books were heaved to the floor that later it was like climbing the Alps to reach the phone ringing on my desk.

There are two windows to my left where I look out on a brick-paved patio. Here I grow oranges, limes, Babcock peaches, and Japanese pears. At times the scent of orange blossoms is so strong the patio smells like the perfume counter at a department store. Beyond, where I've taken up some of the front lawn, I grow figs, plums, apples, tomatoes, and corn. Who says Josh McBroom is a made-up character?

I no longer conjure professionally, but I keep up with the new tricks and sleights and concoct new fooleries of my own. I pal around in this caped world with my magician dentist Dr. Dan Alessini and one of the Magic Castle's star wizards, pickpockets, and scholars, David Avadon. A clutch of magicians, calling ourselves Wizards West, gathers once a month here at the house. We attempt to fool one another.

Some months ago, for example, with a couple of apple trees in the yard, I ordered an apple peeler from Burpee. I immediately saw a trick in it. At the next Wizards West meeting, I had a card selected and had a corner torn off for identification. I made the card vanish. Then I brought out the Rube Goldberg device and put an apple, freshly examined, in it. As I cranked, the apple got peeled, cored, and sliced. When I spread the slices like an accordion, there was a card inside— the selected card. The corner matched.

I explained the secret. I told my fellow wizards that I grew the apple with a card inside. They are a cynical lot. I wonder what Harry Snyder, still in his carnival spats, would have thought. Would he have caught my palming tricks? I sometimes wonder what happened to him. True to his profession, he vanished into thin air.

When I was young, I couldn't seem to think up or find story plots. Now I can sit at my desk without an idea in my head and, like a palming trick, produce a rough plot. I suppose that skill is one of the marks of a professional.

That's not to say I don't miss a lot of story material around me. I remember being with Clyde Bulla in Santa Barbara for a writers' conference and having our shoes shined. A girl of ten or twelve polished them up. I didn't see a story in her. Clyde did. He wrote a novel called *Shoeshine Girl*, one of his most arresting and moving stories.

Since I make few story notes but let ideas buzz around in my head, I write seven days a week. If I take a day off, I feel like a juggler who has dropped all the Indian clubs. And I will have lost momentum. That phenomenal writer Georges Simenon would write a chapter a day until he finished. If interrupted for a day, he abandoned the novel.

Well, I'm not so concentrated, but I understand. I may growl and grumble, but I pick up the Indian clubs and press on with the story. Once the manuscript is finished, I stretch my arms and declare an extended holiday.

See Sid stretch.

I notice that quite often authors' public photographs
show them thirty years earlier, in the prime of youth.
Here I am, taken ten minutes ago.

(Photo credit: Kevin O'Malley)

Books by Sid Fleischman

FOR MAGICIANS ONLY

1939 *Between Cocktails*, Abbott's Magic Novelty Company
1942 *Ready, Aim, Magic!* (with Bob Gunther), self-published
1943 *Call the Witness* (with Bob Gunther), Magic Limited
1947 *The Blue Bug* (with Bob Gunther), Magic Limited
1947 *Top Secrets* (with Bob Gunther), Magic Limited
1993 *The Charlatan's Handbook*, L & L Publishing

MAGIC BOOKS FOR THE GENERAL PUBLIC

1953 *Magic Made Easy*, by Carl March (pseudonym), Croydon
1975 *Mr. Mysterious's Secrets of Magic*, Atlantic Monthly Press

MYSTERY AND SUSPENSE NOVELS FOR ADULTS

1948 *The Straw Donkey Case*, Phoenix Press
1949 *Murder's No Accident*, Phoenix Press
1951 *Shanghai Flame*, Gold Medal Books
1952 *Look Behind You, Lady*, Gold Medal Books
1953 *Danger in Paradise*, Gold Medal Books
1954 *Malay Woman*, Gold Medal Books
1954 *Counterspy Express*, Ace Books
1955 *Blood Alley*, Gold Medal Books
1960 *Yellowleg* (a western), Gold Medal Books
1963 *The Venetian Blonde*, Gold Medal Books

BOOKS FOR YOUNG PEOPLE

1962 *Mr. Mysterious & Company*, Atlantic Monthly Press
1963 *By the Great Horn Spoon!*, Atlantic Monthly Press
1965 *The Ghost in the Noonday Sun*, Atlantic Monthly Press.
      Reillustrated and republished, Greenwillow Books, 1989
1966 *Chancy and the Grand Rascal*, Atlantic Monthly Press
1966 *McBroom Tells the Truth*, Norton
1967 *McBroom and the Big Wind*, Norton
1970 *McBroom's Ear*, Norton

1970 *Longbeard the Wizard,* Atlantic Monthly Press
1971 *Jingo Django,* Atlantic Monthly Press
1971 *McBroom's Zoo,* Grosset
1971 *McBroom's Ghost,* Atlantic Monthly Press
1972 *The Wooden Cat Man,* Atlantic Monthly Press
1973 *McBroom the Rainmaker,* Grosset
1974 *The Ghost on Saturday Night,* Atlantic Monthly Press
1976 *McBroom Tells a Lie,* Atlantic Monthly Press
1977 *Me and the Man on the Moon-Eyed Horse,*
Atlantic Monthly Press
1977 *Kate's Secret Riddle Book,* Franklin Watts
1978 *McBroom and the Beanstalk,* Atlantic Monthly Press
1978 *Humbug Mountain,* Atlantic Monthly Press
1978 *Jim Bridger's Alarm Clock,* Dutton
1979 *The Hey Hey Man,* Atlantic Monthly Press
1980 *McBroom and the Great Race,* Atlantic Monthly Press
1981 *The Bloodhound Gang in The Case of the Crackling Ghost,*
Random House
1981 *The Bloodhound Gang in The Case of the Flying Clock,*
Random House
1981 *The Bloodhound Gang in The Case of the Secret Message,*
Random House
1981 *The Bloodhound Gang in The Case of Princess Tomorrow,*
Random House
1982 *McBroom's Almanac,* Atlantic Monthly Press
1986 *The Whipping Boy,* Greenwillow Books
1987 *The Scarebird,* Greenwillow Books
1990 *The Midnight Horse,* Greenwillow Books
1992 *Jim Ugly,* Greenwillow Books
1995 *The 13th Floor,* Greenwillow Books

COLLECTIONS

1992 *McBroom's Wonderful One-Acre Farm,* Greenwillow Books
1992 *Here Comes McBroom!,* Greenwillow Books